I've seen Rod Parsley in action. He's the real deal—a bold, dynamic man of faith who's committed to doing the right thing no matter what. I've seen him inspire countless others to become more engaged in the political process. This book continues that leadership—it's a proven, winning game plan for the people who became known in the fall of 2004 as "values voters." If more people heeded Rod Parsley's advice, we'd be much better off as a country.

—Ted Haggard, Senior Pastor,
New Life Church
President, National Association
of Evangelicals

I was privileged to travel with Rod Parsley in the fall of 2004 as we made the case with congregations throughout Ohio for a constitutional amendment to defend marriage. His leadership in getting others engaged in the political process is a prime reason the amendment passed handily in our state and ten others that November. This book should inspire men and women of faith to build on those victories and make "values voters" a force that politicians can no longer ignore.

—The Honorable Kenneth Blackwell
Ohio Secretary of State

America's future depends on moral champions like Pastor Rod Parsley. I believe that without his leadership and faith in the Word of our Lord and Savior, we would be in a far worse place today.

— The Honorable Walter Jones
U.S. Congressman, North Carolina

Silent No More is a compelling, must-read book—not just for Christians, not just for church people, but for all Americans. Rod Parsley's writings on judicial tyranny, race relations, poverty, Islam, and other topics are explosive and insightful, and they will move people to action. *Silent No More* was a joy to read, and I highly recommend it to all Americans.

—BISHOP KEITH A. BUTLER
WORD OF FAITH INTERNATIONAL
CHRISTIAN CENTER, SOUTHFIELD, MI

Silent No More will swell the chorus of values-oriented citizens who are striving to take back their country. Rod Parsley speaks out on the major issues that threaten the future of our culture and the long-term security of our nation. *Silent No More* does not merely lay out the scope of the challenge, but also offers the information and action steps essential to the solution.

—THE HONORABLE TONY PERKINS
PRESIDENT, FAMILY RESEARCH COUNCIL

Rod Parsley cuts to the chase like the prophet of old Isaiah. He makes it explicitly clear in *Silent No More* that the Christian must not succumb to the political correctness philosophy but speak with clarity against evil. His facts and analysis make the reality of our coming forth more pertinent.

—REVEREND LOUIS P. SHELDON
CHAIRMAN, TRADITIONAL VALUES COALITION

Like Rod Parsley, my heart often breaks as I think of the moral state of America. Guilty of thinking that no one else cared, I was greatly encouraged by reading *Silent No More*. It was like an injection of liquid hope. Written in a conversational but scholarly style, this book helps to bring understanding and direction for concerned Americans.

Ever wish you had a source of clear biblical answers for the greatest problems of our day? Ever wanted to respond to a negative person with an informed scriptural answer? Then *Silent No More* is a must-read.

—BISHOP HARRY R. JACKSON JR.
SENIOR PASTOR, HOPE CHRISTIAN CHURCH
COLLEGE PARK, MD

SILENT
NO MORE

ROD PARSLEY

Charisma
HOUSE
A STRANG COMPANY

Most Strang Communications/Charisma House/Siloam products are available at special quantity discounts for bulk purchase for sales promotions, premiums, fundraising, and educational needs. For details, write Strang Communications/Charisma House/Siloam, 600 Rinehart Road, Lake Mary, Florida 32746, or telephone (407) 333-0600.

SILENT NO MORE by Rod Parsley
Published by Charisma House
A Strang Company
600 Rinehart Road
Lake Mary, Florida 32746
www.charismahouse.com

Unless otherwise noted, all Scripture quotations are from the New King James Version of the Bible. Copyright © 1979, 1980, 1982 by Thomas Nelson, Inc., publishers. Used by permission.

Scripture quotations marked KJV are from the King James Version of the Bible.

Scripture quotations marked NIV are from the Holy Bible, New International Version. Copyright © 1973, 1978, 1984, International Bible Society. Used by permission.

Quotations from the Quran are from Abdullah Yusef Ali, *The Qur'an Translation*, seventh edition (Elmhurst, NY: Tahrike Tarsile Qur'an, Inc., 2001).

Cover design: The Designworks Group, Charles Brock
www.thedesignworks.com
Cover photography: Better Image
Photography: Greg Bartram
Interior design: Terry Clifton

Library of Congress Cataloging-in-Publication Data
Parsley, Rod.
Silent no more / Rod Parsley.
p. cm.
ISBN 1-59185-659-0 (hardcover)
1. Christianity and culture--United States. 2. Christianity and politics--United States. 3. Church and state--United States. 4. United States--Church history--21st century. I. Title.
BR115.C8P326 2005
261'.0973--dc22
2004025956

05 06 07 08 09 — 9876543
Printed in the United States of America

DEDICATION

"And now abide *faith, hope, love…*"
—1 Corinthians 13:13

To Austin—who every day teaches me what
faith really is

—ᴄ·

To Ashton—who gives me true *hope* for the next
generation of spiritual leadership

—ᴄ·

To Joni—my one true *love*…forever, and the
greatest earthly example of God's unconditional
love I have ever known

—ᴄ·

Like "these three," the three of you abide forever
in my heart and have shown me why God made
families—to bring unimagined joy to every other
aspect of life.

ACKNOWLEDGMENTS

I'm the only person pictured on the jacket of this book, and that's terribly misleading. Any great project requires all kinds of people with diverse talents, and the greatest number of people focused on the smallest point of agreement yields the greatest results. We were focused and in agreement, and it worked. It's an incredible privilege to live and work with people who share my commitment to defend biblical truth and restore our nation's wayward culture.

My heartfelt thanks go out to:

- My parents, James and Ellen Parsley: Who taught me that true morality is doing what is right…right, even when it seems out of step with popular opinion.

- The members and staff of World Harvest Church in Columbus, Ohio: Your generosity in allowing me to travel in support of these issues was overwhelming. I am humbled to be your pastor.

- The voters of the state of Ohio and the nation: Thank you for demonstrating the power of "values voters."

- Ohio's secretary of state, the Honorable J. Kenneth Blackwell: Thank you for your courageous and outspoken support of moral values and for your invaluable involvement during the Silent No More tour. Character like yours is instrumental in restoring honor to public service.

- The Mansfield Group: Battles are won not only by the strategy of generals, but also by the diligent efforts of those who often labor in obscurity, attending to the details that determine the difference between success and failure. Thank you for your encouragement and professional support in this project.

- There are many others who made this book possible, but three deserve special mention: Dr. Dale Berkey; the director of the Center for Moral Clarity, Debbie Stacy; and Senior Elder Bill Canfield: Thank you for your labor, dedication to the cause, and your ability and willingness to translate the language of my heart into words that will stimulate consideration, discussion, and action.

CONTENTS

I swore never to be silent whenever and wherever human beings endure suffering and humiliation.

—Elie Wiesel

Our lives begin to end the day we become silent about things that matter.

—Martin Luther King Jr.

When the eagles are silent, the parrots begin to jabber.

—Winston Churchill

PROLOGUE

It's Showtime
SILENT NO MORE

E ven before November 2, 2004, I knew "values voters" would make a difference in the national election. I didn't know this because I had an overwhelming spiritual experience that gave me inside information from beyond this world. I didn't know it because of what other people told me. I surely didn't know it because of what the media headlines reported. I didn't even know it because of what dependable public officials like Ohio's Secretary of State J. Kenneth Blackwell were saying.

I knew it because I could see it in the people's eyes.

I canceled my fall schedule to tour cities in America on a Silent No More tour. In sixteen meetings within thirty days, I spoke across the country, and especially in my home state of Ohio, making the case for moral values to as many people as would listen. That summer I had founded the Center for Moral Clarity as a way for people of faith to unite and contend with the staggering moral decline witnessed in our culture.

The tour was an eye-opening experience for me and, it seemed, for those attending. In congregation after congregation, as I talked about the terrible toll same-sex marriage would inflict on our culture,

I saw facial expressions change. It was as though scales had fallen from their eyes, and they could finally see the cost of sitting on the sidelines while the political process went forward without them. And even though liberal elitists on both coasts delight in characterizing them as gun-toting, Bible-thumping, knuckle-dragging Neanderthals, they *got it*. And the liberal Left didn't and still doesn't—you might say the Left lived up to their name and left mainstream America behind.

As I returned home from an evening of ministry in New Jersey the night before the 2004 national election, I sensed "values voters" were about to do something historic. The people I had spoken to on the tour—especially in predominantly African American congregations—and the tens of thousands of people who had joined the Center for Moral Clarity in its first four months were going to make a difference in the election that the polls weren't picking up.

And they did! You know the story by now. Evangelical Christians not only turned out at the polls in large numbers, but they also overwhelmingly supported the candidates and issues that best reflected their values. According to the Barna Group, although evangelicals were just 7 percent of the voting-age population, they constituted 11 percent of the voters. Altogether, born-again Christians made up 53 percent of the people who voted in the 2004 presidential election, though they make up just 38 percent of the national population.[1]

My feeling is that people of faith did not so much create a wave as they struck a nerve. Those who supported traditional moral values simply initiated momentum that had been lying dormant, waiting for the right moment. The national spotlight, which had been careening from one crisis to another, fell steadily on moral issues in the aftermath of the election, illuminating some dazzling distinctions. The results may be enlightening or frightening, depending on your perspective.

First, when they finally realized that values for too long taken for granted were under assault, mainstream Americans identified with those values and fought to defend them. The much-misunderstood evangelical voter was not really that far to the right of the majority of Americans—whether those Americans were Jewish, Catholic, or even nonreligious. Some people were astounded to discover that there are plenty of nonreligious folks who have strong, family-oriented values.

Consider the Left-leaning state of Oregon. Not generally known as a bastion of conservatism, more than 150,000 voters who cast their ballot for the Democratic presidential candidate also supported a state marriage amendment prohibiting same-sex marriages.[2] Senator Kerry won the state by less than a 70,000-vote margin,[3] proving that the marriage issue was not what divided the country—on the contrary, it united people who found moral values in common with those of a different political point of view.

Next, the mainstream media demonstrated they are hopelessly, and probably unrecoverably, out of touch with many of the subscribers they say they serve. From months of biased news coverage to election night exit polls, many of the prognosticators and pundits clearly showed they inhabited a parallel universe with only a tenuous connection to the reality most Americans experience.

Finally, the results of this election showed that mainstream America is exactly that—the mainstream. The fringe elements are so far out on the edge that they are in danger of falling off the map altogether. Elitists in Hollywood, New York, and Los Angeles refuse to believe there is anything about them that was repudiated by the majority of voters in places like Nowata, Oklahoma, or Casper, Wyoming. The liberal Left has been fully exposed for its breathtaking intolerance and boundless sense of moral superiority.

Apparently they think the only opinions that have any validity are those espoused by TV or movie personalities, and the rest of us poor, uneducated, unenlightened, unwashed slobs need to take our cues and get our clues from them. Many prominent liberals made now-broken promises to leave the country if the election turned out the way it did. Talk of secession came up in serious conversations—and there has even been a map called "the United States of Canada" (Canada plus the blue states) circulating on the Internet.[4] As for me,

I'm glad to live in an America where individual citizens making up their own minds are still more powerful than billionaires with leftist agendas.

In the 2004 election, eleven states passed constitutional amendments affirming God's desire for marriage—the union of one man and one woman. Six other states had already approved such amendments in the previous months. Once again, in the liberal state of Oregon, where at least one jurisdiction illegally issued marriage licenses to same-sex couples early in 2004, the constitutional amendment passed with a 57 percent affirmative vote. The other ten states all had a winning margin of 59 percent or more.[5]

In Ohio, where I had spent a lot of time encouraging Christian voters to go to the polls, the marriage protection amendment passed with 62 percent of the vote.[6] This was especially gratifying because a number of Ohio lawmakers, newspapers, major corporations, and municipalities publicly opposed the issue. Clearly, most voters in this country—not just evangelicals—want marriage to remain defined as a union between one man and one woman.

What's next? Well, it's impossible to imagine that the battle to protect marriage is over or that it will be easy. Proponents of same-sex marriage will most likely challenge those election results in court. Or they may attempt preemptive legal tactics in other states.

I'm convinced that we must continue an assertive strategy to protect marriage. A Federal Marriage Amendment is absolutely essential to prevent a handful of judges from doing damage to our family structure that could never be fully undone.

And lest we get complacent, "values voters" suffered one significant defeat on Election Day 2004. A California ballot proposal will provide billions of dollars in state funds for embryonic stem cell research for at least the next ten years.[7] We must not be silent on this issue. At this point, incredibly, opinion polls show that most people don't see anything wrong with it! But it's destroying human life in the name of science. Killing a living being is wrong when it is called *abortion*, and it's just as wrong when it is called *research*! We have a great deal of educating to do on embryonic stem cell research, and you can bet we will do it.

California is also where another disturbing state law was passed in 2004. This legislation revised that state's hate-crimes statute to make sexual orientation a protected group whose immorality cannot be criticized—even by our nation's pastors, priests, clerics, and rabbis speaking from the tenets of their faiths. People of faith, including our Center for Moral Clarity, are responding to this misguided legislation. We will not relent until we see changes not only to this law but also to the conditions that led to its enactment.

November 2, 2004, wasn't the end of our fight for a more moral culture. It was the beginning. More than at any time in our country's history, men and women of faith are recognizing their responsibility for the culture they live in and will leave to the next generation. We asked for this moment, and now the spotlight of America's attention is turned toward us. We must speak up for an America based on the foundation our fathers established—a foundation of faith and of commitment to moral boundaries.

We have lost that America. But we can get it back. This is the task we undertake with conviction and confidence. Our times demand it.

—Rod Parsley

INTRODUCTION

The Commitment of Our Fathers, the Calling of Our Times
SILENT NO MORE

I will be silent no more. I must speak, and I must speak now. Our times demand it. Our history compels it. Our future requires it. And God is watching.

For decades, I have labored in Christian ministry across this nation. I have, by God's grace, built a church of thousands and preached the message of Jesus Christ around the world. By the miracle of television, I have taught the truth in millions of America's homes. I have preached in stadiums where crowds gathered hours in advance to hear the answers their souls longed for. I have been privileged to feed the hungry, teach the young, influence the powerful, and stand for righteousness in this land.

But this is not why I speak now.

Nor do I speak because faith has become the consuming interest of our generation. Only the sadly uninformed would fail to know that since September 11, 2001, our country has raised a great chorus of spiritual desperation. In a land where it was once thought rude to discuss religion in public, where men spoke seriously of the death of God, questions of faith now rule the public discourse. From Mel Gibson's film *The Passion of the Christ* to Rick Warren's *Purpose-Driven* books, from the award-winning rock group Evanescence singing, "Wake me up inside, save me from the nothing I've become," to a *Newsweek* cover story asking, "Who Is Jesus?"—our generation is seeking as few others have done in history. Even distortions of the truth, like the popular novels *The Da Vinci Code* and *The Rule of Four,* show that people are grasping for spirituality at any price.

This I know—but it is not why I speak.

Instead, I speak because we have come to a moment in time when the possibilities for this nation are so great, when the crises in this nation are so pressing, and when the voices of wisdom in this nation seem so few that not to speak would be the violation of a sacred trust. Indeed, it may be that now, at the dawn of a new millennium, our nation has the potential to become what our fathers dreamed. But if this is true, it is no wonder that this dream is being attacked from without and dismantled from within. As President George W. Bush said in his moving speech at the National Cathedral just days after September 11, 2001: "The commitment of our fathers is now the calling of our time."[1] He was right. It is time to renew our fathers' commitment. It is time to reclaim our lost heritage, and there is much to be gained by a return to the discarded values of the past. It is time to remake our nation into the just, compassionate, noble society she was meant to be.

I will, therefore, be silent no more.

How can I remain silent when the founding faith of our nation is driven from the marketplace of ideas? How can I sit quietly by while the very words our Founding Fathers intended to protect faith are used to destroy it? Owing to a horrible perversion of language and law, the same First Amendment of our Constitution that bars government from restricting belief has been used to drive Christianity from the national public square. Our society ought to be secular, we are told: no prayer in our schools; no God in our pledges; no faith in our politics. And all this we are to accept from the hands of activist judges who repeatedly overturn the will of the people as expressed through their elected representatives. No, I will not let such outrages go unmarked.

Nor will I stand in embarrassed silence while old faiths and new agendas rush in to fill the void left by a supposedly discarded Christianity. I will rail against the idea that the God of Christianity and the god of Islam are the same being. I will sound the alarm about the agenda of America's tortured homosexuals, about Hollywood's perversion of love and sex, and about the murder of the old and the unborn alike. I will not be silent until the media's high-tech persecution of my faith is exposed and until the very schools my tax dollars support are no longer the enemies of everything I teach my children to believe.

Yes, I know what they will say. They will say that these are the same issues that Bible-thumpers have been complaining about for decades. They will say that religious people care only about protecting their beliefs, but they couldn't care less about society as a whole. But they misjudge me. They do not know where I have been. They do not know what I believe. Nor do they understand that I intend to speak boldly to both sides of the political spectrum: to both the believing and the nonbelieving, to both the socially conscientious as well as the economically conscientious. I intend to take issues that traditionally belong to the Left and commend them to the Right. I intend to take the concerns of the secular and commend them to the religious. In short, I intend to offend everyone. In fact, you might say I'm an equal opportunity offender.

For example, I can no longer sit quietly by while poverty suffocates millions of people in the world's richest nation. I was born to parents who grew up in Martin County, Kentucky, a county so poor that President Lyndon Johnson chose to announce his "war on poverty" there. My parents lived in coal mining camps. Outsiders made fun of us by saying that we lived so far back in the hollows that June bugs didn't show up until August and that we used hoot owls for roosters. They said we were raised too poor to pay attention, but even so, we were taught values in that culture that did not excuse criminal activity because of poverty. We may have been poor, but we didn't steal from anyone or kill anyone because of it.

My father left home to fight in the Korean War. When I was born, my parents were both working—sometimes several jobs each—and often they had no car to get them from place to place. Yet they learned how to trust God. When there was little in the kitchen cupboard and less in the bank, they trusted God. When I was nearly killed by a speeding automobile, they trusted God. When I almost died of accidental poisoning, they trusted God. And they prospered because they worked, they gave, and they prayed. Ultimately, they broke that cycle of poverty in our family.

I want you to know, though, that my family will never forget what it means to be poor. I will tell you from experience that grinding poverty sucks hope from the human soul, that haunting lack unchallenged by faith gives rise to fear and bitterness. This ought not to be in our land of plenty. And sadly, while the political Left offers only the strained resources of the state, and the political Right feels obligated only to offer the poor a level economic playing field, the church sleeps on. Yet a serious commitment by this generation of Americans to their less fortunate brothers and sisters could mean the end of poverty in our time. Can I fail to speak the truth?

Nor can I be silent in the face of the rushing tide of racial hatred in our land. It is a serious indictment of those who lay claim to biblical truth that Sunday morning is the most racially segregated time in America. It is an indictment of our culture that young black males are more likely to be shot, imprisoned, unemployed, or killed by disease than any other group in America. Recent surveys show that racial hatred is not on the decline among youth in America; it is on the rise. This is not a liberal issue. It is not a conservative issue. It is an issue for patriots, for those who believe in an America built on the content of a man's character rather than the color of his skin.

Painful as it may be, I also cannot refrain from confronting the materialism of our age. We are swimming in a culture of debt. We are drowning in an unrestrained lust for more toys. Who hasn't endured the annoyance of this scenario or one just like it: A balding man with a bulging paunch drives a yellow convertible in a vain attempt to relive the glory days of his youth. As a high school football star, he really believed if he would have just had that car, he would have surely gotten that girl. The more we have, the more we want, and it is robbing us of peace, robbing us of community, and robbing us of any higher meaning for our lives. The things we demand and the debt we are willing to tolerate to have them are creating a bondage our children and our grandchildren will be forced to confront decades from now. This is as true for the nation as it is for the family. Should I not point out the nobler way?

I know also that some will say that I never have been silent. "How can this man say he will be silent no more?" they will ask. "He has never stopped talking!" There is a very good reason for this. Shortly after I was born, the doctor who delivered me told my mother about a serious birth defect—it seems I was born without a mouth. The doctor assured her it would be no problem to give me one, but he needed some direction about its size. My mother, groggy from medication, said, "Put it from about *here to here,*" indicating with her finger where it should go. The doctor misunderstood and instead of giving me a mouth that went from here to here, gave me one that went from *ear to ear.*

But, you see, for the most part I have been speaking to the Church. Even when I spoke of the broader matters of our nation, I spoke to the Church. I knew the Church held the answers. I knew that the Church was the sleeping giant that could transform our nation if only she would break out of her prisons of style, prisons of personality, prisons of tradition, prisons of flawed theology, prisons of powerlessness, and—dare I say it—prisons of cowardice. I have spoken to the Church because the ancient words tell us that judgment begins with the house of God (1 Pet. 4:17). I have spoken to the Church, and I will continue to speak to the Church. In fact, many have said that when it comes to speaking my mind, I have a bad case of the "can't help its." Now, though, I must speak also to the nation as a whole. I must speak to those whom the Church does not reach and for whom the voice of the Church is tragically silent.

I must say too that I do not intend to offer mere high-minded platitudes and the kind of sweeping statements most people expect of a man who preaches on television. Instead, I intend to teach you. I intend to challenge your mind. I intend to work you. Sometimes in this book I will show you the shape of the forest. But sometimes I'll make you work through a thick patch of trees. In other words, I'm going to show you the factual basis of the things that I say. This will take some patience on your part. It will take some effort. But we aren't going to change our generation with opinions. As you know, opinions are like noses—everyone has one, and some are bigger than others. Some time ago, my son spoke up (as always seems to be the case) in front of some people I was attempting to impress and said, "Wow, Dad, you really have a big nose!" But it is important that our opinions, whether big or small, are informed by facts. It is time that we stop being a mile wide and an inch deep, that we reach our intellectual roots into the deep soil of truth to produce the cultural fruit our generation desperately needs. I don't apologize for writing a book that requires thought, reflection, and maybe even the rereading of a page or two. Isn't the good of our nation worth the effort? I say it is.

Because I believe this, I am going to end each chapter with *Action Points*, practical steps you can take after you absorb the truth on each topic. During World War II, Winston Churchill issued orders to his staff on notepaper that was headed with the words, "Action This Day." Because he insisted on immediate, meaningful action, he moved the British government toward victory rather than allowing it to languish in bureaucratic stagnation. I hope you will take "Action This Day" after you read each chapter. Remember, this book isn't designed to move you to think great thoughts. It is designed to present thoughts that lead to actions, the kind of actions that will transform our country.

So now you understand: I can be silent no more. Not until the land of our fathers' dream arises. Not until we become the truly kind and noble society we were fashioned to be. Not until the commitment of our fathers truly does become the calling of our times.

There is a chance for a great and righteous nation to emerge in the years ahead. I pray for it. I hunger for it. I long for our children to know it. And now you understand why, until that land of promise emerges...

I will be silent no more.

CHAPTER 1

JUDICIAL TYRANNY:
The Genius of Our Fathers,
the Folly of Our Times

SILENT NO MORE

> The Constitution is not an instrument for govern-
> ment to restrain the people; it is an instrument for
> the people to restrain the government—lest it come
> to dominate our lives and interests.
>
> —PATRICK HENRY

You have surely heard all the horror stories. Like me, you have probably shaken your head in dismay, prayed to God for mercy, and wondered where it all would lead.

Remember?

A court in California rules that requiring students to say the Pledge of Allegiance with the words "One nation under God" is a violation of the First Amendment. I can deal with the kind of misunderstanding the first grader had when he raised his hand to ask his teacher a question after reciting the words "one nation under God, indivisible..." in the Pledge. "Teacher," he asked in all earnestness, "why does God make our nation invisible?" What I have trouble with is federal judges who have an even greater misunderstanding. A public school teacher is chastised for keeping a Bible on her desk and reading it during her lunch hour. A president who publicly declares his belief that all men are created by God is accused of violating the "separation of church and state." A gifted student is denied a state scholarship he earned because he wants to use the money to attend a Christian seminary. On and on it goes.

The problem is that none of this squares with the legacy of our Christian Founding Fathers. Because of the foundation of faith they set for us, we have chaplains in the military, chaplains in Congress, and even chaplains in federal prisons. The artwork and inscriptions on our federal buildings in Washington DC scream of a Christian heritage, and prayers are heard at the start of cabinet meetings, sessions of Congress, and even the start of a Secret Service detail's day. When the multiple tragedies of September 11, 2001, occurred, senators and congressmen who once sought to safeguard the separation of church and state stood shoulder to shoulder on the steps of the U.S. Capitol and sang "God Bless America."

It is all very confusing to most Americans. We watch the courts issue rulings that seem at odds with the underpinnings of the American dream. Yet we want to trust the wisdom of judges and those in authority over us. Still, because we don't tend to know much about our history, we let myths that are repeated often enough take on the assumed authority of fact. And nowhere in American life do myths dress up like facts as much as they do in the question of religion in our national life.

For example, ask the average man on the street in America what the Constitution has to say about religion and government, and he is going tell you that the Constitution requires a separation of church and state. It has the ring of truth to him because these words have been repeated so often. But they are false. The Constitution says nothing about the separation of church and state. In fact, the Constitution never mentions the word *church*. Instead, these words were first used in a private letter that Thomas Jefferson wrote to a group of Baptist ministers in Danbury, Connecticut. They have entered our laws and our culture over time, but they aren't in the Constitution.

Moreover, Thomas Jefferson wasn't even in the country when the Constitution was written. He was our ambassador to France at the time. The words did appear in a constitution once, though: the old constitution of the Soviet Union. I don't think we want to model ourselves on that disastrous experiment!

So, myths abound, and in the meantime, the founding faith of our country is banned as a ruling force in our culture. This is despite the fact that a *Time* magazine poll in June of 2004 reported that more than half of Americans believe that: "We are a religious nation, and religious values should serve as a guide to what our political leaders do in office."[1]

Something is seriously wrong, and I want to help you understand what it is. I would like to take you back in our history for a moment and visit again what our Founding Fathers believed about religion and politics. This is much more important to me than the lunatic fantasies of some Hollywood has-been or Nashville retread trying to give us their wisdom on public policy. Then, I would like to scan how our courts have done violence to that original intent and left us with the cultural mess we have now. Once that is done, I want to discuss some solutions, because my point here isn't just to complain. My point is to launch a movement of moral clarity to reclaim our country.

ORIGINAL INTENT MADE CLEAR

There really isn't much question about what the Founding Fathers intended regarding the relationship between religion and government. Those who talk about how complex the matter is, or how our founders weren't clear, either want to use an assumed confusion to take us down the road of secularism, or they are just ignorant. Either way, they ignore the wisdom that shouts from the pages of history.

Let me give you an example of how easy it is to see what the Founding Fathers intended. It was during the summer of 1787 that an august body of our early leaders met in the Pennsylvania statehouse to devise what came to be known as our Constitution. The story of that convention is fascinating, and I hope you will read some of the great accounts of that famed moment in our history in books like Catherine Drinker Bowen's *Miracle in Philadelphia*.

On July 13 of that epic year, when the convention was but seven weeks along in its great task, a Christian minister named Rev. Manasseh Cutler interrupted the flow of business to ask a simple question: "What is required to earn congressional approval for the settling of a new territory?" Cutler wanted to establish a colony in the Ohio territory, and there were others besides him who wanted to move beyond the original thirteen colonies to settle territories further west. What were the requirements going to be? What standards did they have to observe to be an official territory of the United States?

The convention's answer became what is known to history as *The Northwest Ordinance of 1787*. It is a fascinating document, and I hope you will find time to read more about it. For our purposes here, though, I want you to notice what the convention said in Article 3. Remember now…the same men who wrote our Constitution wrote these words. Here is Article 3.

> Religion, morality, and knowledge, [*sic*] being necessary to good government and the happiness of mankind, schools, and the means of education, shall forever be encouraged.[2]

The words are almost hard to believe, aren't they? The men who wrote the Constitution actually believed that religion is essential to good government—not a hindrance to it, not a perversion of it, and not betrayal of it. Rather, they said that religion is "essential" to good government. What a stark contrast to the whimpering, dribbling, and verbal tap-dancing we hear today on this issue.

But that's not all. They also said that *morality* is essential to good government, a concept that is almost foreign to many of our government leaders today. What's more, they said that they thought *religion* was essential to the happiness of mankind. Even the notoriously deistic Benjamin Franklin asserted, "I have lived, Sir, a long time; and the longer I live the more convincing proofs I see of this Truth, that God governs in the Affairs of Men. And if a Sparrow cannot fall to the Ground without his Notice, is it probable that an Empire can rise without his Aid?"[3] When was the last time you heard someone in Washington DC talking about what makes people happy, much less about how religion is essential to real happiness? Finally, notice that the men in Philadelphia didn't make the above statements in general. They made these statements by way of saying that schools should be built to make sure religion, the kind of religion that builds a good society and makes people happy, should always prevail in America.

It's really pretty simple, isn't it? The men who designed our government made it very clear that they thought religion was essential to the success of the Republic. Was this all they said? Was this one isolated statement? Not at all.

While in Congress, John Adams wrote in a letter to his wife, "Statesmen may plan and speculate for liberty, but it is religion and morality alone which can establish the principles upon which freedom can securely stand."[4] In this, Adams reflected a firmly held and much loved idea of his day, one that could be heard echoing from every pulpit, classroom, and printing press in the land. In fact, the president of the convention himself, George Washington, would later write that "of all the dispositions and habits which lead to political prosperity, Religion and morality are indispensable supports."[5] Significantly, the framers did not regard religion merely as a tool of government for placating the people. Instead, they believed that government, as they conceived it, could not function successfully on any foundation other than a religious one. For them, government was the external expression of the internal moral force of religious truth. James Madison expressed this popular sentiment powerfully in words attributed to a speech he made in 1778:

> We have staked the whole future of American civilization, not upon the power of government, far from it. We have staked the future... upon the capacity

of each and all of us to govern ourselves, to sustain
ourselves, according to the Ten Commandments of
God.

Undoubtedly, most of the members of the Constitutional
Convention would have agreed with Madison and could easily have
written Adams' famous words, "Our constitution was made only for
a moral and religious people. It is wholly inadequate for the government of any other."[6]

It is hard to understand how anyone could miss what our Founding Fathers intended. It seems beyond question. Yet even secularists
will agree that men like Washington, Adams, and Madison were pri-
vately Christian with a Christian vision for the nation. What these
secularists maintain, though, is that when the framers wrote the First
Amendment, they specifically made provision for a secular government. This is what many Americans believe today, and this is the
basis of a large number of court rulings. It doesn't seem to matter that
nothing could be further from the truth.

THE FIRST AMENDMENT

Let's find out what our Christian Founding Fathers really intended.
When the Constitution was nearing completion, some in the country
were concerned that certain individual liberties had not been suf-
ficiently outlined. There was debate about whether this was so, but
finally the framers decided to add a Bill of Rights to the Constitution.
This Bill of Rights was comprised of ten amendments, the first ten
amendments of the more than two dozen we now have. What we want
to examine further is the First Amendment of this Bill of Rights, for it
contains the only mention of religion in the entire Constitution.

You have to remember that the men of the revolutionary era had
just separated from England, and they did so in large part because
King George was trying to force the English state church on the
American colonies. The great evangelist George Whitefield had
warned the colonists of this Anglican threat to their religious liber-

ties. It was his revival preaching from Georgia to Massachusetts that unified the colonists both in faith and in vision. Because our colonial forebears would not submit to King George's control of their religious lives—among other tyrannies—the American Revolution was, in part, a holy war. This is why British troops often killed colonial pastors, burned colonial Bibles and hymnals, and turned colonial churches into riding stables or houses of prostitution.

The men who wrote the Constitution and added the Bill of Rights to it wanted to make sure that a state church could never again be forced upon the people. This was obviously the reason for the First Amendment. We can see this concern in the suggestions for the Amendment proposed by the various states. As one scholar has written, "These suggestions clearly indicated that the states wanted to prevent the establishment of a national religion or the elevation of a particular religious sect to preferred status as well as to prohibit interference by the national government with an individual's freedom of religious belief."[7]

For example, the Maryland Ratifying Convention proposed an amendment stating, "That there be no national religion established but that all persons be equally entitled to protection in their religious liberty."[8] The Virginia Convention proposed a similar approach in Article Twenty of its famous "Declaration of Rights":

> That religion, or the duty which we owe to our Creator, and the manner of discharging it, can be directed only by reason and conviction, not by force or violence; and therefore all men have an equal, natural, and unalienable right to the free exercise of religion, according to the dictates of conscience, and that no particular religious sect or society ought to be favored or established, by law, in preference to others.[9]

Like wording is found in the proposal of the New York Convention: "That the people have an equal, natural and unalienable right freely and peaceably to exercise their religion, according to the dictates of conscience, and that no religious sect or society ought to be favored or established by law in preference to others."[10] The resolutions of Maryland, Virginia, and New York are typical of the resolutions of other states, such as North Carolina and Rhode Island.[11] In each case, it is clear that the intention of the resolution is to prevent Congress from establishing a national church or from preferring one religious sect over another, thus inhibiting the individual's freedom of religious practice.

Though James Madison did not believe that a religion amendment was necessary, since no power had been delegated to the federal government to establish a national religion, it is obvious that the wishes of the state conventions were not lost on him, for his initial draft of the First Amendment read: "The Civil rights of none shall be abridged on account of religious belief or worship, nor shall any national religion be established, nor shall the full and equal rights of Conscience be in any manner, or on any pretext, infringed."[12]

While Madison's draft was considered by a select committee, of which Madison was a member, the Senate version emerged from debate on September 3, 1789. It initially read: "Congress shall make no law establishing one religious sect or society in preference to others, or to infringe on the rights of conscience."[13] After continued discussion, however, it was changed to read: "Congress shall make no law establishing religion, or prohibiting the free exercise thereof."[14] The wording was changed to its current form by a joint committee, which also included Madison, so that it read: "Congress shall make no law respecting an establishment of religion or prohibiting the free exercise thereof." The House accepted this version on September 24, 1789, and the Senate accepted it on the next day.[15]

THE FOUNDING GENERATION

I have recounted all this to show that what the First Amendment was intended to do was to prevent Congress from ever establishing a state church. No one wanted a secular state. In fact, a secular state had never even existed before, nor would it until the final stages of the French Revolution. The Founding Fathers wanted the citizens and states of America to be as religious as they wanted to be, but they wanted Congress to stay out of the church business.

This isn't to say, though, that they wanted America's statesmen to keep religion at arm's length. In fact, the very men who framed our government were so overtly Christian that they would drive today's advocates of secularism out of their minds.

How can I be sure of this? Just listen. In 1789, the same year in which Congress approved the First Amendment, James Madison served on a committee that approved congressional chaplains. Madison also recommended days of thanksgiving at the behest of Congress on four separate occasions. Though as president, Thomas Jefferson objected to nationally sponsored days of prayer, he nevertheless recommended to Congress in 1803 a treaty with the Kaskaskia Indians, which included a yearly federal stipend of $100 for seven years to support a Catholic priest. Other treaties like this were enacted—with Jefferson's support—with the Wyandot Indians in 1806 and with the Cherokees in 1807. Similarly, in 1796, Congress ordained special lands for the use of Christian Indians in an Act entitled "An Act regulating the grants of Land for propagating the Gospel among the Heathen."[16]

Let's be clear here. I'm describing what the men who wrote the First Amendment did when they were in government. They printed Bibles. They funded chaplains. They called the nation to prayer and fasting. They even funded missionaries to the Indians. This sure doesn't sound like a secular state to me. It sounds like a Christian nation honoring the gospel but without creating a state church.

If all this isn't proof enough, though, look at the father of our country, George Washington. His behavior most typifies the broad interpretation of the First Amendment, which was prevalent at the time. As president, Washington proclaimed days of thanksgiving, frequently spoke in churches, prayed at public occasions when a chaplain was not available, and invoked the name of God in public pronouncements.[17] During his presidency he addressed Dutch Reformed, Protestant Dutch, German Lutheran, United Baptist, Presbyterian, Methodist, German Reformed, Episcopal, Congregational, Swedenborgian, Quaker, United Brethren, Universalist, and Jewish meetings.[18]

Washington was so outspokenly Christian that the Presbyterian Church sent an address to him declaring that they "esteemed it a peculiar happiness to behold in our Chief a steady, uniform, avowed friend of the Christian religion; who has commended his administration in rational and exalted sentiments of piety; and who, in his private conduct, adorns the doctrines of the gospel of Christ; and on the most public and solemn occasions, devoutly acknowledges the government of Divine Providence."[19] What a contrast to another former chief executive carrying a big family Bible down the church steps for the world to see while having a sexual affair with an intern and then publicly lying about it. Clearly, Washington saw nothing in his actions that he believed would violate the First Amendment.

Even more astonishing is that during the administrations of all of the early presidents, the federal buildings in Washington DC were used as churches on Sundays. No one thought this at all strange or in any way a violation of the First Amendment. It is certainly ironic, given some of the Supreme Court rulings of recent years, that the original room where the Supreme Court met in the U.S. Capitol was regularly used for church services on Sundays and when the Court was not in session.

There is simply no question about it. The founders of our country wanted religion, which would have meant Christianity in those days, to shape our national philosophy and institutions, but they did not want the Congress to ever create a state church. They did, however, want government to encourage religion in general and to enable religious institutions to further the good of the country.

WHAT WENT WRONG?

So, if this interpretation of our early history is so very obvious, how have we ended up in the crisis we are in? How did such a plain intent on the part of our fathers become the justification for a secular society?

Let's go back again into history. The turning point begins, quite innocently, just after the Civil War. When Congress was attempting to grant the freed slaves their full rights, it passed the Fourteenth Amendment. This amendment simply stated that no state could deny a citizen rights he or she had under the federal Constitution. This is, of course, what had been happening under the slave system. Slaves weren't granted any rights as citizens. After the war, Congress wanted to make it clear that freed slaves were citizens and that no state could decide to deny former slaves or anyone else the rights that the Constitution gave them. This meant that the states were bound by the Constitution in a way that they hadn't been before. Remember that the Constitution originally only pertained to the federal government.

All of this was good except for one thing. What about the First Amendment? Did Congress intend for the Fourteenth Amendment to mean that the First Amendment applied to the states as it did to the federal government, that the states had to stay away from religion and from encouraging religious practices? This was important, for some states were far more overtly religious than the federal government. Most states made strong Christian statements in their state constitutions and sponsored deeply religious schools. Some of them even had requirements that people running for office had to be Christians and believe in the truth of the Bible.

To find out what Congress intended, a congressman named James Blaine introduced a resolution in 1875 stating that the Fourteenth Amendment was intended to apply the First Amendment to the states. Blaine was trying to force the issue and make Congress be clear about what it was intending.

Now let's be very clear about what was happening. Congress had passed the Fourteenth Amendment. This amendment applied the federal Constitution to the states. Before this, the Constitution had defined the federal level of government but not the states. So the question arose as to whether Congress intended the states to become as religiously constrained as the federal government had been. If Congress said yes, that it did want the First Amendment to apply to the states, then decades of legal precedent would be overturned and many state religious practices would have to end.

Congress gave its answer. It rejected the Blaine Amendment. Congress clearly wanted the states to be as religious as they wanted to be. What is more, Congress not only defeated the Blaine Amendment in 1875, but it also considered and rejected the Blaine Amendment or similar proposals that would have had the same effect at least twenty-five times between 1870 and 1950.[20] Clearly, Congress wanted to prevent a national church but allow the states to be as religious as their citizens wanted them to be.

Now, why is all this important? It is this: though we have seen that neither the Founding Fathers nor the generation of statesmen who ratified the Fourteenth Amendment ever intended to ban religion from being an influence on our government or from shaping our culture, it was exactly these men that the Supreme Court cited to begin removing faith from our public life. As astonishing as this is, given all the history we have just reviewed, the founding vision of our nation was somehow interpreted by the Supreme Court to deny a vital role for faith in the fashioning of public policy.

I have made such an almost outlandish claim here that I have to back it up. Let's go back to 1947. The case of *Everson v. Board of Education* came before the Supreme Court. The issue was simple, really: a school district in New Jersey had begun reimbursing parents for the costs of transporting their children to religious schools. It seemed only fair, since the school district made contracts for the transportation of children to public schools, that those who went to private religious schools should be reimbursed for the same kind of transportation.

The practical issue before the Court was not what made the case such a turning point in our history. It was, instead, the way that the court decided to interpret the law. Remember, now, what we have seen in our scan of history:

1. Our Founding Fathers wanted to prohibit a state church but also wanted to encourage religion in general.

2. The words "separation of church and state" do not appear in our Constitution.

3. The application of the Fourteenth Amendment to the states was never intended to mean the application of the First Amendment to the states, meaning the states could be religious if they wanted to be.

With these realities in mind, listen to how the U.S. Supreme Court ruled in the *Everson* case. Writing for the majority, Justice Hugo L. Black asserted that the First Amendment erected "a wall of separation between church and State" which "must be kept high and impregnable."[21] The religion clauses were intended, he wrote, "not only to keep the states' hands out of religion, but to keep religion's hands off the state, and above all, to keep bitter religious controversy out of public life by denying to every denomination any advantage from getting control of public policy or the public purse."[22]

Justice Black's words are an amazing reinterpretation of both our law and our history. Listen to his conclusion, though:

> The "establishment of religion" clause of the First Amendment means at least this: Neither a state nor the Federal Government can set up a church. Neither can pass laws which aid one religion, aid all religion, or prefer one religion over another. Neither can force nor influence a person to go to or to

21

remain away from church against his will or force him to profess a belief or disbelief in any religion. No person can be punished for entertaining or professing religious beliefs or disbeliefs, for church attendance or non-attendance. No tax in any amount, large or small, can be levied to support any religious activities or institutions, whatever they may be called, or whatever form they may adopt to teach or practice religion. Neither a state nor the Federal Government can, openly or secretly, participate in the affairs of any religious organization or groups and vice versa. In the words of Jefferson, the clause against establishment of religion by law was intended to erect "a wall of separation between church and State."[23]

Despite our history, our founding faith, the evolution of our laws, and the will of the people, the Supreme Court laid the foundation for a new vision of America—a secular and antireligious vision. Justice Black's conclusion is that the America of Washington, Jefferson, and Adams cannot be and will not be the America for you and me. According to the Court, religion may no longer shape our public life. Faith is private, something that should never influence our laws and our national vision. From this case, over the course of years, came the removing of the Ten Commandments from state buildings, the removal of prayer from the public schools, the challenging of Bible clubs and religious instruction on state school campuses, and the whole trend toward *neutralizing* our governmental institutions from religious influence.

In fact, had the Court's ruling in the *Everson* case been the law of the land in the early days of our country, most of the Founding Fathers would have been in violation of it, a good number of government's religious efforts would have been deemed unconstitutional, and our national life would have taken on a very different character. Indeed, it might not be overstating the case to say that some of our nation's greatest leaders—President Washington, for example—might have landed in jail. The *Everson* case was, simply put, a travesty of law and a corruption of history. Surely Thomas Jefferson himself would have been astonished to witness how his words had been twisted.

So now we live in a society in which atheists file lawsuits to have "In God We Trust" erased from our money, in which the American Civil Liberties Union (ACLU) challenges almost every expression of our Christian heritage, and in which "faith-based initiatives"—of a kind our Founding Fathers enacted themselves—are considered by some legal minds to be a violation of the law. Simply put, we are watching the banishment of our heritage.

DEFEATING JUDICIAL TYRANNY

I know I paint a depressing picture. I know too that much of the picture is bleak. But I have not brought you to this point in an understanding of our nation to leave you with defeatist attitudes. Let me explain.

First, I want you to be encouraged by how clear our Founding Fathers were on the issue of religion. Their lives speak for themselves, and the more people who come to know their story and their ideals today, the more hope we have for a restoration of the original intent of the founding generation.

Second, I want you to realize that it has been only a matter of decades since the Supreme Court ruled in the *Everson* case, essentially making Thomas Jefferson's phrase "separation of church and state" the law of the land. It is possible for this ruling to be overturned. It is possible that our children may one day look back to the last half of the twentieth century as a time when the intentions of our Founding Fathers were perverted just before a great movement in our country insisted that this perversion be reversed. In other words, just as slavery was eventually outlawed after being sanctioned by the laws of the land for decades, so the perversion of the First Amendment may well be corrected, particularly since it has only been the law for just over fifty years.

Finally, I want to talk to you about one possible way this correction could take place. Not long ago I visited our nation's Capitol and toured the room where the Supreme Court met in the early days of our country. It was a revelation. The original room where the Supreme Court convened was nearly in the basement of the U.S. Capitol. In fact, I was told that the whole issue of where the Court would meet was actually an afterthought.

You see, the Supreme Court was not that important as an institution under the original understanding of the Constitution. The Court simply ruled on the constitutionality of the matters referred to it. The Court did not make law or have many of the powers it has today. Not until the advent of some of the cases you studied in school—like *Marbury v. Madison* and *McCollough v. Maryland*—did the Court grant itself the powers of judicial review.

In fact, our Founding Fathers would be shocked to see the power the Supreme Court has today and to know that the justices think nothing of making law. This was never the proper function of the Court. When the Court ruled in the famous *Roe v. Wade* abortion case of 1973, Justice Brennan admitted that the Constitution did not address the issue of abortion directly, but said that the Court's ruling was derived from the "emanations of the penumbras of the law." What in the world does that mean?

"Watch out for those who use fifty-cent words," an elderly acquaintance once told me, "because they may be as phony as a three dollar bill." Clearly, we have moved away from the literal meaning of law and moved to what scholars call "legal realism" or "sociological jurisprudence." This means simply that the law is whatever the judges say it is, because the judges are no longer bound by the literal meaning of the law. Some call this *judicial tyranny*.

Think about what this is doing to our country. Despite what our Founding Fathers intended or even what elected legislators determine, one judge can make a novel ruling never before hinted at in the law, and it changes the course of the country. One judge, perhaps a very liberal member of the ACLU, can bend the law to his or her philosophy, and, because we are no longer anchored to the original intent of our Constitution's framers, this innovative ruling becomes the law of the land, or at the least it becomes a point of departure for other rulings.

This is such an important point that I want to give you some examples. You know that the issue of homosexual marriage is a much-contested issue in our society. Just let me give you a little background on this situation. The people of Massachusetts voted into law a state regulation that prohibited the establishment of same-sex marriage, but the liberal judges of their Supreme Court decided to ignore the will of the people. On November 11, 2003, Massachusetts' highest court struck down the ban on same-sex marriage as unconstitutional, a move that has the potential of effectively destroying the institution of the family in America if you and I don't act now. Our Constitution rightly requires that a marriage recognized in one state must also be recognized in every state of the union. This means that a handful of robed radicals are thumbing their noses at six thousand years of Judeo-Christian values and deciding the fate of our entire nation, despite the will of the people.

So watch what happened. Gavin Newsom, the newly elected mayor of San Francisco, allowed four thousand homosexual couples to be married in the city despite California's law, which defined marriage as "between one man and one woman." Soon after, the California Supreme Court ordered Newsom to stop, but not before he had emboldened other mayors to follow his rebellious lead.

Among them was Jason West, the mayor of New Paltz, New York, who began marrying homosexual couples despite a New York State law that, like the California law, defines marriage as the union between one man and one woman. West said he had an obligation to break the law and that, regardless of the criminal charges—a nineteen-count misdemeanor indictment—he had no intention of stopping his illegal conduct. Others followed his example. Portland,

Oregon, began allowing same-sex marriages, which led to more than two thousand same-sex couples exchanging vows.

These people are lawbreakers, and somebody needs to say so. I believe the only thing that can save marriage in America is an actual amendment to the Constitution of the United States that will forever define marriage as the union of one man and one woman, as God intended it, thus stopping this kind of judicial tyranny in its tracks.

Let's look at another issue: the way one judge overturned the Partial-Birth Abortion Ban Act of 2003. Think about it. A president is elected for a term of four years—eight, if the people choose him for a second term. A senator serves for six years at a time. A member of the House of Representatives serves for two years per term. Federal judges are not elected at all. They are appointed, and the term of their service is for life. Once they make a ruling, it becomes the precedent for all similar cases and has the effect of the rule of law.

Sometimes this has disastrous results. The Partial-Birth Abortion Ban Act was a marvelous piece of legislation. I had the privilege of being there when President Bush signed it into law. It was an act that expressed the will of Congress, the people, and, of course, President Bush. To help you understand how important this legislation was, let me include some of the language here. It reads:

> A moral, medical, and ethical consensus exists that the practice of performing a partial-birth abortion—an abortion in which a physician deliberately and intentionally vaginally delivers a living, unborn child's body until either the entire baby's head is outside the body of the mother, or any part of the baby's trunk past the navel is outside the body of the mother and only the head remains inside the womb, for the purpose of performing an overt act (usually the puncturing of the back of the child's skull and removing the baby's brains) that the person knows will kill the partially delivered infant,

performs this act, and then completes delivery of
the dead infant—is a gruesome and inhumane procedure that is never medically necessary and should
be prohibited.

Rather than being an abortion procedure
that is embraced by the medical community, particularly among physicians who routinely perform
other abortion procedures, partial-birth abortion
remains a disfavored procedure that is not only
unnecessary to preserve the health of the mother,
but in fact poses serious risks to the long-term
health of women and in some circumstances, their
lives.[24]

You see why this law was so important. Babies were being murdered after they were partially brought into this world. The law
put a stop to it. Then came Judge Phyllis Hamilton, a liberal judge
appointed to the bench by President Clinton. Single-handedly, Judge
Hamilton ruled the Partial-Birth Abortion Ban Act unconstitutional.
She said that the Act poses "an undue burden on a woman's ability
to choose a second trimester abortion," that it is "unconstitutionally
vague," and that it lacks a valid health exemption for the mother. You
know what else she said? She ruled that it is "irrelevant" whether the
baby suffers pain in the process of a partial-birth abortion.

Just so you don't think this is some abstract legal matter, let me
get painfully specific. Hold your nose for a moment and read Judge
Hamilton's description of partial-birth abortion.

A D&E abortion is a surgical procedure, which is
performed in two steps: dilation of the cervix and
surgical removal of the fetus.... This process usually
causes the fetus to disarticulate.... Some physicians
puncture the calvarium and suction out the cranial
contents, others disarticulate the calvarium and
crush it with forceps before extraction, while yet

others use forceps to collapse the calvarium while
it is still attached.... Fetal demise can be effected in
a number of ways, and it can take up to five to ten
minutes for fetal demise to occur.[25]

Now, let me put this language in simple, graphic terms. I'm not
doing this for fun. I am doing it because you have to understand
how critical these issues are. Listen to what the above paragraph
actually says.

The cervix is artificially opened, and the unborn
child is extracted. This usually causes the baby to
be dismembered. Some abortionists stab the baby
in the skull before sucking out its brain, others pull
the baby's head off and crush it before taking it out,
and others crush the skull while it is still attached to
the baby's body. There are a number of ways to kill
an unborn baby, and it can take five to ten minutes
for the baby to die.[26]

You see what has happened here. One judge issuing one ruling
contrary to the will of the people and their leaders means that babies
die—and die horribly. This is judicial tyranny.

Now, I told you I thought there was a solution. There is. Do you
know that the Constitution grants authority to Congress to determine
what kind of cases the judiciary, meaning the courts, can hear and
what kind it cannot? It is true. The Congress can tell the courts that
there is a whole category of law it does not want the courts involving
themselves in. They have done it before—and more than once. For
example, around the time of the Civil War, Congress stated in a case
called *ex parte McCardle* that it did not want the Supreme Court to
hear cases relating to slavery. Congress was wrong to do it, but this
episode in our history nevertheless shows what is possible.[27]

Suppose our current Congress decided that the courts have made
enough of a mess out of the issue of religion in our public life or out

of abortion and homosexual marriage laws. Suppose a decision was made that First Amendment issues—and the abortion and definition of marriage issues that spring from religion—should only be decided by elected legislators. If Congress would exercise its power to restrict judicial review, it could tell the judiciary to stay away from cases that pertained to these matters and leave them only to the lawmakers elected by the people. Then you wouldn't have one judge in California deciding that a reference to God in the Pledge of Allegiance violated the Constitution or that babies should die half born or that two men can be married. You would instead have those issues decided by the legislature of California or, ultimately, by Congress. At least these decisions would be in the hands of lawmakers elected by the people and accountable to them at the next election. I think this would be a huge correction to the distancing of the courts from the original intent of the Constitution.

What I want you to leave this chapter with is the belief that the trends of the last decades can be changed. We can reclaim the nation our fathers envisioned. We can start a grassroots movement that induces our elected leaders to assert themselves over the courts. And we can make sure that the present generation understands anew the beauty and genius of the founding generation. But it will only happen if you who have read this chapter, if every pastor who understands these issues, and if men and women of goodwill who are devoted to this nation are willing, like me, to be silent no more.

ACTION POINTS

- Vote for candidates who will appoint and confirm judges who believe in original intent and who have high moral standards.

- Support legislation to limit the time for consideration of federal judgeship appointees so that they cannot be kept in limbo indefinitely without a confirmation vote.

- Contact your congressmen, and ask them to support HR 235, the Houses of Worship Free Speech Restoration Act, which was introduced to liberate clergy from the muzzle imposed by an absolute ban on all speech that might be regarded as "political," and thereby enable them to speak out on all vital, moral, and political questions of the day. It would free houses of worship from the fear, anxiety, and uncertainty created by the threat that the IRS might impose financial penalties or revoke tax-exempt status. For more information on this vital legislation, log on to the Library of Congress' legislative Web site http://thomas.loc.gov and enter the name of the bill in the blank provided.

- Visit David Barton's wonderfully insightful Web site www.wallbuilders.com.

- Recommended reading:
  Courting Disaster: How the Supreme Court Is Usurping the Power of Congress and the People, by Pat Robertson[28]

Chapter 2

RACE:
Fulfilling Our Fathers' Dream
SILENT NO MORE

> My part is to help speed the day, now fast approach-
> ing, when there shall not be a Northern heart and a
> Southern heart, a black heart and a white heart, but
> all shall be melted by deeds of sympathy, patience,
> and forbearance into one heart—the great Ameri-
> can heart.
>
> —Booker T. Washington

In the Library of Congress there hangs a painting that was intended to capture the founding vision of America. It is called *The Dawn of the Millennium*, and it is one of the most amazing paintings I have ever seen. Let me describe it to you.

In the center of the work is an altar mounted on a hill in what is clearly intended to be the lush, fruitful, untainted landscape of America. Standing around the altar, which glows with the glory of God, are ministers from every Christian denomination. Those who know the style of the time can discern leaders of the Presbyterian, Congregationalist, Quaker, Catholic, and Episcopalian churches. The picture suggests that one purpose for America is to be a place of God's presence that brings unity to all the varying streams of Christendom.

Yet there is more in the painting. At the feet of these Christian leaders, a child plays beside a lion. This is obviously a reference to the great prophecies of Isaiah that peace will rule on earth one day. An African slave is shown also, now free and standing nobly erect rather than bent over his work. If you look beyond the altar to the distant hills, you will see symbols of the nations drawing near. There are turbaned Arabs and Native American Indians and discernibly Asian figures all drawing near to the altar of the Lord.

This was indeed the founding vision of America. Men dreamed a dream from the heart of God. America would be a land so permeated by biblical truth and righteousness that the glory of God would dwell here, unity would reign, the nations would come, and the world would see a model of Christian civilization as it had never seen before.

This dream lived in the hearts of the first Pilgrims, who wrote in their journals that they sailed to the New World, in part, to introduce the natives of this land to the Prince of Peace. When they arrived, not only were they rescued by the famed Indians Squanto and Samoset, but also they treated the natives of the region with great kindness. The dream also lived in the heart of John Winthrop, leader of the Puritans, who preached in his famous sermon "A Model of Christian Charity" that this land was to be a "city upon a hill." He too believed that God intended this land to be a place of religious unity and racial harmony in service to the cause of Christ worldwide.

This was the dream of our founders, and it was a dream from God. But it did not prevail long. You see, not everyone who settled America was intent upon the glory of God. Some came for wealth, and some came to escape the fruit of their past vices. Some came merely to wield power, and some came to build for their own glory. Motives like these distorted men's souls and refashioned the lush provision of God in the New World into mere tools for their own schemes.

It did not take long for these lesser motives to prevail in our history. Soon the very Indians whom our Christian forebears yearned to befriend and convert were treated as enemies to conquer and contain. In fact, some of the greatest injustices in American history were committed against the Native Americans, yet we, as a nation, like to pretend nothing ever happened. Even today we ignore the facts that Native Americans have some of the highest alcohol dependency rates in this nation. In 2002, this group reported the highest rates of substance dependence or abuse. Yet, what American, if asked on the street, could tell you that? Recently, we have made efforts to acknowledge the misdeeds of our past and work toward a better tomorrow. The opening of the Smithsonian National Museum of American Indians as well as legislation now under consideration in Congress, which would issue an apology from the United States government to the American Indians, are enormous steps toward setting this country back on course.

Of course, we cannot forget how our forefathers soon transformed the lives of Africans by selling them in the marketplace to work the land as the property of Christian owners. It seems, early in our nation's history, that the dream of a land in which the diverse races of the world could live in a righteous, respectful harmony started to die. Our forebears soon began questioning whether black men had souls and whether Indians could be converted. So began the legacy of racism in America, as old as human sin and as tragically destructive as the histories of the great civilizations reveal—all in contradiction to the glorious vision of our founding.

I remember my first journey to the Deep South. We took a family vacation in the mid-1960s, and my parents, my sister, and I piled in an old Buick and headed for what seemed to me a foreign country. I remember seeing cotton fields being picked by African Americans, including very small children. I noticed their fingers and hands bleeding, and I wondered how they were able to stand under the scorching sun for so many hours. I thought of how it made the back of my legs ache when I bent over to pick green beans in my parents' garden, and I could not imagine how those people must have felt after laboring in the fields day after day.

I remember stopping at a service station along the highway (this was in the day when they actually provided service) and seeing the signs on the three restrooms in the back of the building. They read, "White Men," "White Women," and the third was designated by only one word, beginning with an "N." This was my introduction to racism in America.

The Scene Today

Now, many years later, we comfort ourselves that things are far different. America has been changed by the Civil War, the Civil Rights Movement, and equal opportunity legislation. As I write these words, George W. Bush is president, and his cabinet is the most diverse in American history. Clearly, nonwhites have ascended to most of the premier positions of power in our land.

Yet I am still sadly forced to report that racism is far from dead in our country. How I wish I could say otherwise. How I wish I could report that we had learned from our tragic legacy of race hatred, that we had heeded the words of William Wilberforce, Abraham Lincoln, Booker T. Washington, Martin Luther King Jr., and hundreds of others who have called us to a higher vision.

Instead, I am forced to report that racism is alive and well in America. We all know it is true. The Ku Klux Klan still exists, black men have been dragged behind pickup trucks to their deaths within the last decade, and a Neo-Skinhead Movement has kept the fires of race hatred burning in this country. Federal programs like affirmative action have done some good but have also engendered deep resentments. We have only to look at the legacy of the O. J. Simpson and Rodney King incidents to see that we have not come as far as we might have dreamed.

I cannot fail to mention, also, that Sunday morning is still the most racially segregated time in America. I must say that if it is true that as the churches go, so goes the nation, we are in trouble when it comes to matters of racial harmony. There are very few thoroughly integrated churches in America when you consider them as a percentage of the total number of congregations in the United States. I am privileged to pastor a church that is highly diverse, with thousands of blacks, whites, Hispanics, and Asians worshiping together passionately. In fact, some people describe our congregation as one of blacks, whites, and Hispanics dancing side by side in their happy stockinged feet. This is the reality in my church, but I am not fooled into believing that this is the norm in our nation.

So I must say that there is an unfulfilled mandate in this area of race. We have not arisen to our destiny as a nation, and we never will as God has defined our purpose, until we see the forces of animosity and hatred and the walls of division destroyed by the crush of righteousness and love. This is not just a vision for the churches, although the churches will have to lead the way; it is a vision for the nation as a whole.

I cannot stress enough how urgent this need is. Do you realize how our population is changing? Hispanic birthrates are five times that of blacks and nearly one and a half times that of whites in this country.[1] In one hundred years, my great-grandchildren may well live in a largely Hispanic America. With increasing immigration to this country, with the birthrates as I've reported them, and with the white population ever decreasing through abortion and purposefully low birthrates, our country will have to learn racial harmony and respect, or we will have a future filled with the violent race wars the skinhead groups now angrily predict.

I have tried in this book to make my case from the founding vision of our nation rather than from Scripture. I know that people expect a pastor like me to lace every point with Bible verses, and I have refrained so I can appeal to a broader audience. But please allow me for a few moments to show you how a vision for racial unity grows organically from Scripture. I must do this, since it is Scripture that has for so long been distorted to make a case for the very racism that threatens to ruin our country.

THE BIBLE UNPERVERTED

It would seem that no one could ever make a case from the Bible for hating a man because of his color. The kingdom of God is so powerfully depicted as a celebration of God's glorious human diversity that it is hard to understand how some have distorted that message. Unless someone tries to make a peculiar case for racial division or slavery from an obscure passage about Ham, Shem, and Japheth deep in the Old Testament, I cannot find anything that supports hating or separating from a man because of his race. Clearly, racism defended with the Bible is a perversion of truth.

When I open my Bible, I find a vision for racial unity springing from almost every page. Not only is it obvious that God created every race and color to reflect His glory, but He even told His "chosen people," the Jews, that they were meant to show the nations God's glory.[2] In other words, the Jews were chosen in part because God wanted them to draw others to Him. This is why God said that the "strangers" who "carried captive his forces," and the "foreigners" who "entered his gates and cast lots for Jerusalem," would find deliverance on Mount Zion, just as His chosen people the Jews had "drank on My holy mountain."[3] Jerusalem was meant to be the United Nations of the kingdom of God.

When I look to Revelation 5:9, I see that Jesus died for every "tribe and tongue and people and nation." His Church was meant to represent this redemptive activity, for even the Great Commission given to the Church in Matthew 28:19–20 was a plan for men of one tribe to go to other tribes and teach them how to reach still others. If Christians lived the Great Commission, churches would be the most racially diverse places on earth.

I know this last statement is radical, so let me give you an illustration. Have you ever looked at the Bible's description of the church of Antioch from a racial perspective? The leadership of that church is described in Acts 13:1. Here is what it says.

> Now in the church that was at Antioch there were
> certain prophets and teachers: Barnabas, Simeon
> who was called Niger, Lucius of Cyrene, Manaen
> who had been brought up with Herod the tetrarch,
> and Saul.

Now, this is just the kind of list most people casually skip over in the Bible. But look at this one closely. Remember that these people were the leaders of a Christian church. Consider: Barnabas, we are told in Acts 4:36, was a Jew from the island of Cyprus. Simeon was apparently black, the name *Niger* meaning "the black." Lucius was from the African region of Cyrene, though we don't know what his color was. Manaen was a Greek who grew up in a future king's home. Saul was from Tarsus in what is now Turkey, then known as Asia Minor.

So notice that among the pastors of the church in Antioch there was a Cypriot, a Greek, two Africans, and an Asian. This diverse team of men led a church in a region that is now part of Syria, yet none of them were from that region. This means that the church at Antioch was led by a multiracial, multinational team, none of whom were local. What an amazing example of the kind of church that the Great Commission should produce!

The Displeasure of Our God

I also want you to get a sense of the way that racism angers God. If we could allow this reality to sink into our souls and into the soul of our nation, it would transform our culture. So let me take a moment to show you an example in the Bible of how racism angered Jesus, and then we will return to the question of racism in our society.

In the Gospel of Mark, chapter 11, we have the amazing story of Jesus clearing the temple. You probably know this tale well. Jesus entered the temple area and noticed that men were exchanging money, selling sacrificial animals, and carrying merchandise through the temple courts. Immediately, Jesus began driving these men out while proclaiming, "My house shall be called a house of prayer" (v. 17).

Throughout the history of the Church, some have concluded that Jesus was upset with merchants doing business in a holy place. There is certainly some truth to this, but it is not the whole story. Allow me to suggest another interpretation. Those merchants were doing business that the law of God required. A man who was going to tithe had to change his local currency into the temple currency. A man who lived far away from Jerusalem was not required to bring the animals he wished to sacrifice with him. He could simply carry money and then buy the sacrificial animals when he arrived at the temple. So, the business we see happening in the temple courts was allowed if it was conducted honestly. It may have been that the merchants were cheating their customers—Jesus did say that His Father's house was made a "den of thieves"—but this may not be the only reason Jesus got so angry.

I think there was another reason Jesus became enraged. I think that Jesus may also have been grieved because the merchants had set up business in the courts, which were the only places that the Gentiles had to pray. You may remember that there was a part of the temple called "The Court of the Gentiles." It was here, according to tradition, that the merchants did their business.

This would mean, though, that the merchants were interfering with the worship of the Gentiles. It is most likely that they were doing this because they despised the Gentiles and thought them unclean and unworthy of consideration in a temple built by Jews. In other words, they were being racists. When Jesus saw the racial callousness of the merchants, He became angry and drove them out while quoting from Isaiah 56. These words are extremely important. We often remember that Jesus said, "My house shall be called a house of prayer." He actually said, "My house shall be called a house of prayer *for all nations*," and He assumed that the Jews who heard him, people who knew their Old Testament very well, would know the context of the passage He was quoting. Let me quote it here.

Foreigners who bind themselves to the LORD
    to serve him,
to love the name of the LORD,
    and to worship him,
all who keep the Sabbath without desecrating it
    and who hold fast to my covenant—
these I will bring to my holy mountain
    and give them joy in my house of prayer.
Their burnt offerings and sacrifices
    will be accepted on my altar;
for my house will be called
    a house of prayer for all nations.
—ISAIAH 56:6–7, NIV

It is clear that Jesus was not only upset about dishonest business being conducted around the temple, but He was also upset about the racism of the merchants who kept the foreigners they so despised from approaching the courts of the Lord.

I will end this brief Bible study by saying that we need a restoration of this kind of holy fire in our churches. By this I am not talking about spiritual excitement, but I am talking about a passion to reflect the passions of Jesus. The angriest moment in Jesus' life was when He railed against racism. Suppose the 82 percent of the American population who say they believe in God, and the half of that number who say they are evangelicals, began to seriously live out the anger of God toward racial hatred. It would transform our nation. This is why I have taken the time to look at just a few of the scriptures that reveal God's heart about race. A perversion of Scripture has justified most of the racism and slavery that has marred our country. My hope is that the true sense of the Bible on race might help drive such heresy from our national life.

The reason I am so desperately concerned about race in America is, as I have said, that America will not fulfill her destiny unless she heals the racial breach and becomes the light to the nations, the example to the world she was made to be. This means not only removing race hatred from our hearts but also refusing to be satisfied until there is not one race in this country that is without equality of opportunity and equality of support from a caring society.

Some will hear me saying something different from what I intend. Some will hear me saying that everyone ought to be equal in every way, that there ought to be no social or economic differences among us. This, of course, is not what I am saying. Only a socialist would say such a thing, and I am the furthest thing from a socialist possible. I am, however, a Christian who believes that our society will be great to the extent we embrace the ethics of Jesus and care for its members as a holy obligation. When any race is left lagging behind their more prosperous brothers and sisters and no one turns to reach for them, then our society is guilty of a callous disregard for the best it is called to be.

BLACKS IN AMERICA

Let me take as an example the condition of a people who are still without the good that other races enjoy. Let me talk about African Americans for a moment. Despite the fact that slavery was ended a century and a half ago, and the battles for civil rights were decided fifty years ago, there is still a horrible disparity between blacks and whites in America. The statistics are staggering.

An African American baby is twice as likely to die at birth as a white baby. The African American mother is four times more likely to die giving birth to that child than an Anglo mother. If that baby survives, he or she is four times more likely to live below the poverty line. If that African American is male, he is six times more likely to be murdered and many times more likely to die of a heart attack, be imprisoned, be unemployed, be a victim of violence, and/or be falsely accused of a crime than a white male. Even successful blacks do not fare as well as successful whites. The median income of a white college graduate in America is $59,914. The median income of a black college graduate in America is $45,079, which is a 24.8 percent difference.[4]

These are distressing facts, but they are not the only issues that concern me about blacks in America. I'm also concerned about a kind of religious racism that is allowing cults to carry away African Americans at an astonishing rate. Let me take a moment to explain what I mean.

The fastest-growing religion is the world is Islam. In America, the fastest-growing religion is Mormonism. Both of these religions are perversions of truth. You will see what I mean in the chapter on Islam we will come to a little later in this book. What is so incredibly sad is that both of these religions are finding tremendous inroads into the black community in America.

That Mormonism is growing rapidly among blacks is surely one of the greatest evidences of spiritual deception and desperation in history. I won't go into the background and perversions of Mormonism, but suffice it to say that if there are any people who ought not to convert to Mormonism, it is blacks. Why? According to this religion, founded by Joseph Smith in the early 1800s, Jesus and Lucifer are brothers. Now this doctrine is strange enough, but what is even stranger is Joseph Smith's belief that Lucifer is the father of the black race. That's right: Mormonism was established, in part, upon the belief that the black race on earth is descended from Satan. And the Mormons didn't disavow this belief until 1974! Still, Mormonism is growing among blacks in America faster than among any other race. What a cruel irony that blacks are now embracing a religion that once viewed them, literally, as children of the devil.

Then there is Islam. Not only is traditional Islam growing among blacks—and largely because blacks are being told that Islam was their original African religion—but an American offshoot of traditional Islam is having a huge impact on blacks in this country. It is called the Nation of Islam, and it is led today by Louis Farrakhan.

The Nation of Islam was founded by Elijah Muhammad in the 1930s. This religion is a strange combination of superstition and borrowings from traditional Islam. It teaches that blacks were the original people on earth and that the first white man was created in a failed science experiment. The world will return to black rule, but only if blacks get out from under white domination, separate themselves from the white race, and reclaim their control of the earth. You can get a sense of this movement from Spike Lee's movie *Malcolm X*, which skillfully portrays how the doctrines of the Nation of Islam appealed to a troubled black youth.

The film also portrays Malcolm X's disillusionment. His hero, Elijah Muhammad, proved to be a hypocrite who fathered children by women other than his wife and who approved of violence. In fact, it was because Malcolm X separated himself from the Nation of Islam and began to move toward traditional Islam that Elijah Muhammad had him killed. In the same way, many blacks today are also becoming disillusioned with the movement and its leader, Louis Farrakhan. Though a powerful speaker, Farrakhan shows signs of imbalance. He believes, for example, that he was once taken up in a spacecraft and interviewed by aliens.

What appeals to so many blacks about the Nation of Islam are some of the good things it teaches blacks to believe about themselves: that being black is nothing to be ashamed of, that blacks are a good and noble race, that the path to power is moral purity, that the black soul has been tortured by racism in America but the damage isn't permanent, and that blacks have a glorious destiny as a people. These are truths the Christian Church ought to be teaching, and when it doesn't, the Nation of Islam fills the vacuum. The problem is that this cult draws well-meaning blacks into layers of deception that lurk just beneath the veneer of truth.

What grieves me so deeply about blacks flocking into any version of Islam is that they are embracing the very religion that enslaved their forebears. Now, I know that this is often due to the failure of the Christian Church to teach blacks the truth about themselves, and I will come to this in a minute. The failure of the Church, though, does not excuse the fact that a serious deception has fallen upon some blacks, a deception that I think makes a mockery of the suffering of their ancestors.

Let me come back to the statement I just made: Islam was the original slave religion. Though there is no question that Europeans extended the evil trade, the truth is that Muslim slave traders were the first to introduce slavery into Africa. Of course, there had always been a kind of tribal slavery in Africa, whereby a defeated tribe would be enslaved by its captors. This was normal at that time in almost every culture of the world. I am referring to the development of a nonmilitary slave trade. This was unquestionably introduced into Africa by Arab slave traders who would hire kidnappers and even pay tribal chiefs to yield up members of their tribe into bondage. Race-based chattel slavery was invented by Islam.

Now you understand why I grieve when a fine young black man is told that his native religion is Islam. When he takes on an Arab-sounding name in an attempt to reclaim what he thinks is his heritage—for example, Lew Alcindor taking the name Kareem Abdul Jabbar or Cassius Clay taking the name Muhammad Ali—he is actually taking on the trappings of the very religion that first enslaved his people. I can certainly understand what this black man seeks to do, and I applaud it. He is trying to make a genuine connection with his African heritage rather than the history of abuse and hate his people have known in America. He is reaching for nobility and authenticity, and we can all understand why. Yet, because the Christian Church has not told the whole story, this young man is left believing that Islam is his heritage and, thus, his destiny. As Karl Marx said, "A people without a heritage are easily persuaded."

I want to tell this young black man the truth. I want to acknowledge the history of slavery and racism in this country, but I also want to tell him that the hardships his people have suffered can serve to make him great. This is, after all, what the famed black leader Booker T. Washington taught his people. He said that slavery was horrible, but that it may have been a tool in the hand of God to position the black people to change the world through forgiveness, righteousness, and industry. I want my young black friend to know the lessons Booker T. Washington had to teach, because I want him to know that the hardships he and his people have suffered can now make them mighty on the earth.

I also want my young black friend to know that it is a lie that Islam is his historic faith, but that I understand why he leans toward believing it. The Church has not given him any sense of heritage in the way it teaches the Bible or relates the history of Christianity. Any young black man who wants to understand why God made him black so he can live out his calling is going to be sadly disappointed when he walks into the average Christian church. He is going to be told of a white Jesus, who is often blond-haired and blue-eyed, and who led a group of disciples who look as if they were born in London rather than Jerusalem. He is also going to be told that Christianity quickly moved out of the Middle East and into Europe where real Christian civilization took root.

Nothing could be further from the truth, and I want my fictional young black friend—and, indeed, all blacks everywhere—to know it. The truth is that Jesus looked more black than white. He was born in the Middle East, for heaven's sake. He wasn't born in Sweden! His skin may have been as dark as many American blacks are today, and His disciples would have been the same.

Yet skin color isn't the main issue. Jesus could have been purple, and it would not have changed the fact that the story of Christianity has belonged as much to Africa as it has to any other continent. Think about it. The Bible tells us it was a black man who helped Jesus carry the cross. Then there was a black man among the pastors of the church at Antioch, the first great missionary-sending church in Christian history. The Ethiopian eunuch took the gospel to his country and sparked a movement that changed that nation forever—again in Africa.

Many of the early Church fathers were African. The brilliant theologian Origen was an African. Anthony, the earliest of the Desert Fathers who did signs and wonders in Egypt, was an African.

Athanasius, who practically stood alone against the world to preserve the doctrine of the Trinity, was not only an African, but he was also nicknamed the "Black Dwarf." And the father of Western civilization, Augustine, was an African born into the home of a Nubian mother and a Carthaginian father. In fact, many of the great movements of Christianity originated on what later became insultingly known as the "dark continent." Many today do not know that the greatest library in the history of our faith was at Alexandria before it was destroyed in a fire by Muslim invaders. The bottom line is that while the ancestors of many whites were still wearing bearskins in the British Isles, there was a sophisticated Christian civilization throughout much of Africa that thrived until it was largely destroyed under the sword of Islam in the seventh and eighth centuries.

What I want the black youth of America to know is that their native religion, the faith that made their continent great until a false religion prevailed, was Christianity. The religion of Jesus isn't a white man's religion. In fact, it belongs more to people of color than it does to whites if we are simply talking about the skin color and nationality of those who first launched it.

You see, then, why it grieves me deeply when a young black man in America finds no sense of connection to a "white gospel" and turns to Islam. He is being denied his true heritage, denied the path to liberation, and deceived into believing that he should take the true religion of slavery as his own. This is the worst kind of religious racism, and the time has come for the truth to set a generation and a race free—once and for all.

POSSESSING THE FOUNDING DREAM

I have been talking about black America. Now I want to talk to black Americans and, for that matter, to all nonwhites in this country. I think what I am about to say may well keep us from destructive divisions and from the loss of our heritage as Americans.

There is a view of the founding of America that leaves a bitter taste in the mouths of nonwhites and, indeed, in the mouths of many in our present society. It goes something like this: The Founding Fathers of America were rich, white racists who compromised the soul of America. They fought a revolution not to launch a righteous nation but to preserve their social class, and they traded on the souls of Africans to do it. The good things about America arose despite them much later in history, and we owe them little by way of respect.

The problem with this view, of course, is that it is not only uninformed, but it also creates a class of people who despise their national fathers and thus distance themselves from the founding faith. By hating what gave them birth, they become a people without a heritage, and, to quote Marx again, "A people without a heritage are easily persuaded." Such thinking has made many in America immune to the wisdom of the Founding Fathers and susceptible to manipulation and radicalism. It has also made them bitter.

Before I go further, let me admit what should be admitted. Our Founding Fathers did not apply to people of color the same belief in the equality of all men that they applied to whites. They did compromise on race—they did not apply the lofty promises of the Declaration of Independence to blacks, and they left our nation exposed to the threat of civil war. Some of them owned slaves. Some were out and out racists. And some died never dreaming that America would be anything but a slaveholding nation. These things are true, and they cannot be denied. Yet they are not the whole truth, and those who think they are risk misaligning themselves with the great destiny of this nation.

What we must also know about the founding generation is how ahead of their time they were and how they formed the foundation for the freedoms we all enjoy today—black, white, Asian, Hispanic, or Arab. Remember that when our Declaration of Independence was penned, most of the world practiced slavery in some form. Blacks enslaved blacks in Africa. Arabs enslaved Africans and took them to the far reaches of the earth. Asian monarchs routinely enslaved their people, and all of Europe dirtied their hands in the vile trade. America was no exception. Still, many of our Founding Fathers realized that slavery could not last, that a great nation could not embrace such a practice forever. This is why many of the framers of our Constitution freed their slaves either during their lifetimes or upon their deaths.

The truth is that the founding generation of America was a transitional generation. They understood that the old ways of the nations could not create a free society, but they did not step as fully as we might have wanted into the values of a modern free republic. They dreamed of a society of free people. They dreamed of a righteous republic modeling liberty for the world. They dreamed up a federal system that has survived for centuries. But they were not as progressive on social issues as we like.

We should be careful to not blame them, therefore. They were far ahead of their time, and we are wrong to charge them with wrongdoing simply because they did not have a twenty-first-century mind-set. Thank God they did not, or they would not have created the wise, largely fair, strong governmental system that they did.

What is more, those who have benefited from the battle for civil rights in the last decades should not reject the heritage they have from the founding generation. They should celebrate it. It was the legacy of that generation that provided the basis for all the freedoms they now know. Think about it. Rights the Founding Fathers could barely envision—like voting rights for women, citizenship for blacks, voting rights for blacks, and property rights for all—were based on the dream of principled freedom our Founding Fathers first handed to us.

So, I say all this because I believe, as I have said from the beginning in this book, that our generation has an opportunity to fulfill the glorious dream of its founding. But it will never happen if a huge portion of our society—the descendants of slaves, people of color, women—views that founding dream as the enemy, as a bondage to escape rather than a legacy to extend. To my black, Asian, Arab, and Hispanic friends, I say, please, have done with bitterness. You live in a great land founded by flawed people who nevertheless framed the liberties you now enjoy. Don't hate them, and don't discard their legacy. Embrace them, and build a nation even better than the one they envisioned. That is what they would have wished for us. We need you, and we need you rooted in the rich soil from which our republic sprang. Remember what Winston Churchill said: "If we open a conflict between the present and the past, we may lose the future."

Now is the time for you to stand tall in the beauty of who you are, hold tightly to the wisdom of our fathers, dream the big dreams of a righteous America, and make yourself and your generation a solemn promise: "I will be silent no more."

Action Points

- Overcome racial barriers by purposefully reaching out to someone from a different race or cultural or ethnic background. Initiate a conversation with them—you might be surprised to find there are more similarities between you than you could have imagined!

- Encourage leaders in your church to share services with another congregation that has a different ethnic makeup.

- Find out information on race at the Coalition on Urban Renewal and Education (CURE) at www.urbancure.org.

- Recommended reading:
  Before the Mayflower, by Lerone Bennett, a history of blacks in America[5]

  Then Darkness Fled: The Liberating Wisdom of Booker T. Washington, by Stephen Mansfield[6]

CHAPTER 3

POVERTY:
The American Century: A Golden Age?

The federal government must and shall quit this
business of relief. To dole out relief is to administer
a narcotic, a subtle destroyer of the human spirit.

—FRANKLIN DELANO ROOSEVELT

Why does poverty continue to be a plaguing problem in this, the
richest nation the world has ever known? Why are there still
hungry children? Why are there families who have no home? Why is
there still a permanent underclass in this great land?

These are the kinds of questions that should drive our national
debate and inform our public policy. As a leader in my community
and in this nation, these are the kinds of questions I have to ask
myself every day. In fact, these are the kinds of questions I grew up
asking as a child raised in a financially struggling home. I remember walking home with my sister from elementary school to find a
grandparent helping out, or at times to an empty house while my
parents both worked two jobs to make ends meet. We did not understand the economic forces that were at work in the nation or the
world that forced them to do that—indeed, we weren't even aware
of them. We knew our parents loved us desperately, and our Mimi

was the best grandmother a child could ever have, but even so, questions would inevitably arise: When would Mama be home? Why did Daddy have to work so long? Are we having potato pancakes *again*? Having faced these questions as a child increases my determination to provide answers.

By all counts we should be emerging from a kind of cultural golden age. It seems that whatever could go right for us has. Over the course of the past two decades, the United States has enjoyed two of the longest peacetime economic expansions in history—and it has enjoyed them virtually back-to-back. Consider:

- This growth alone has been greater than the size of the entire German economy. Inflation dropped from 15 percent to 3 percent.

- Interest rates fell from a high of 21.5 percent to 6 percent.

- Twenty million new jobs were created.

- Exports surpassed those of both Germany and Japan.

- Our share of worldwide manufacturing output rose for the first time in forty years.

- American innovators led the world in the most critical high-technologies—computer microprocessors, silicon chips, fiber optics, digital displays, software, and Internet protocols.[1]

Internationally, the American vision succeeded beyond our wildest dreams. Who could have ever imagined that Poland, Hungary, Czechoslovakia, Romania, and Bulgaria would shake off the shackles of communist tyranny without reprisals from Moscow; that Germany would tear down the Berlin Wall and reunite under a democratic government aligned with the West; that South Africa would move steadfastly toward some formula for universal enfranchisement; that the old realms of Croatia, Slovenia, Lithuania, Estonia, and Latvia would emerge phoenixlike from the ashes of totalitarianism; that even the Soviet Union would literally come apart at the seams and then cease to exist altogether; and that the war on international terrorism would be engaged with such stridency and apparent success? Yet within the span of just a few years—a single lifetime—this is precisely what has happened. The Cold War is over. The enemies of freedom now can only lurk in barren mountain hideaways, spider holes, and stark bunkers on the opposite side of the planet. We have emerged as the sole remaining superpower.

In 1941, Henry Luce prophetically announced the "American Century."[2] In 1988 George Bush reiterated that prophecy—and then claimed that "the best is yet to come. The American Century has not drawn to a close."[3] He later went on to boast, "No one—no one in the whole world doubts us anymore."[4]

No one, that is, except us. Just when everyone else suddenly believes in us, we doubt ourselves. As renowned British historian Paul Johnson has said, "A paradox now faces the United States, one that is glaringly apparent to a regular visitor like me. A majority of its inhabitants are enjoying a material prosperity unprecedented in history. Yet our [sic] nation is nonetheless tormented by ferocious self-doubt and self-criticism, and even by a sense of failure and doom."[5] Pogo Possum, a well-known comic strip character of yesteryear, put it succinctly when he paraphrased a famous quote this way: "We have met the enemy, and he is us."

Perhaps this grim outlook exists because all Americans have not enjoyed the benefits of our great prosperity in equal—or even proportionate—measure.

The dark specter of poverty continues to stalk this great land of freedom, prosperity, and opportunity. Virtually unaffected by the erratic cycles of boom and bust, recovery and recession, its shade continues to haunt big cities and small towns, suburbs and farms, ghettos and rural communities, in both good times and bad. Jesus said, "The poor you will always have with you" (Matt. 26:11, NIV). American history seems to provide poignant evidence that Jesus was right.

Several concurrent trends have emphasized this more than ever before: the feminization of poverty, the farm crisis, AIDS displacement, and the health-care crunch.

Evidence everywhere abounds. More than 70 percent of women in the labor force today work out of economic necessity. More often than not, they are single, widowed, or divorced. And more often than not, they are poor. An astonishing 75 percent of this nation's poverty is now borne by women and their children.[6]

The number of poor families headed by men has actually declined over the past fifteen years by a little more than 25 percent. Meanwhile, though, the number of poor families headed by women has increased nearly 40 percent. As a result, poverty is becoming more and more a phenomenon of single women and their children.[7]

The fact is the liberalization of divorce laws, the elimination of preferential treatment in the workplace, and the escalating crisis in women's health care—which I'll discuss in a later chapter—have left women more vulnerable than ever before to the ravages of poverty.

But poverty is not just an urban concern. According to the Census Bureau, only about 14 percent of this nation's poor live in the decaying inner cities. Another 47 percent live in large metropolitan areas. But all the rest—a frightening 39 percent of the total poor population—live in rural regions. Those nearly fourteen million poor Americans are our farmers, ranchers, loggers, hired hands, and migrant harvesters.[8]

All across the vast and fertile Farm Belt is mounting alarm that the grim harvest of failures and foreclosures that have threatened the family farm with extinction over the last decade will continue indefinitely. The American farmer is facing the fiercest crisis in fifty years—since the end of the Second World War. Almost half a million farms are currently threatened with bankruptcy. Nearly 72 percent of all persons occupied with full-time agriculture have had to resort to some sort of federal welfare assistance, and the numbers grow with every passing day.[9]

Precipitated by a number of ill-advised political moves—artificial price support programs for farm commodities, easy-to-get federal land bank loans, billions in farm subsidies, and protectionist trade policies—the farm crisis had reached a fever pitch by the end of the eighties, leaving thousands, perhaps even millions, of rural families utterly destitute. Matters have only gotten worse since.

I live in a city. Probably you do, too. But as I travel over one hundred nights per year speaking, what I see and have become all too aware of is the poverty that is wracking the rural communities of our world today may seem very remote to us until we visit our local grocery store. It is at that point that we should all realize how much we depend on the farmers of this nation. It is these farmers, as I have said, who are in the most desperate crisis of their lives. Yet, what attention does their situation get?

Then there is the AIDS crisis. According to the Centers for Disease Control in Atlanta, the number of reported AIDS cases among "at-risk communities" continues to grow at an alarming rate despite all the attention it has received. This astonishing rate is now doubling every twenty months. And the number of people actually infected with the deadly virus may be "one hundred times higher than that of reported cases of AIDS." This means that as many as four million people in the United States may have AIDS.[10]

Medical care for each one of those patients ranges anywhere from seventy-five to two hundred thousand dollars, only a tiny fraction of which can be feasibly covered by Medicaid or other social welfare programs.[11] Couple that stark economic reality with the fact that AIDS patients are considered pariahs in the workplace and thus spend their final months, or even years, unemployed, and the destitution of a vast proportion of our population becomes a foregone conclusion.

Although research in this area remains somewhat scanty, it appears that more than half of all AIDS patients fall below the poverty line within six months of their diagnosis. Nearly one-third wind up homeless, living in welfare hotels, public shelters, charity hospices, or even on the streets.

All talk of the AIDS crisis naturally segues into a discussion of the health-care crisis. There are plenty of good reasons why cries for compassion to the poor and demands for health-care reform are so closely connected. According to statistics compiled by the World Health Organization, the picture is indeed dismal.

- Nearly a quarter of all Americans are uninsured.[12]

- Half of those uninsured live below the poverty line.[13]

- About one-fifth of them are impoverished children.[14]

- Another one-fourth are elderly—living on less-than-adequate fixed incomes.[15]

- Infant mortality rates are rising dramatically—especially among the disadvantaged.[16]

- A quarter of the unborn are "substance exposed," which means their mothers abused drugs while they were pregnant.[17]

- As many as one-eighth of all school children are not immunized.[18]

- Nearly one-fifth of all factory workers remain uninsured.[19]

Sadly, it doesn't take a catastrophic illness to plunge most American families into an economic crisis—just a persistent health problem can do the trick.

POVERTY:
The American Century: A Golden Age?

When you add the crises of women in poverty, farm failures, AIDS, and inadequate health care to the permanent underclass of the welfare culture, is there any wonder that in this day of booming prosperity, there is more than a little sense of ill ease?

THE ALMS RACE

In his State of the Union message of 1964, President Lyndon Johnson declared an "unconditional war on poverty."[20] Almost immediately, the full energies of the most powerful nation on earth were marshaled against poverty. Studies were authorized. Commissions were established. Images of Appalachian shanty towns and ghetto hovels filled America's television screens. A helter-skelter of ambitious programs was launched. Governors and mayors set out on hopeful pilgrimages to Washington to lobby for their "fair share."[21] The federal coffers were loosed. The alms race had begun.

The "war on poverty" was supposed to reform the entire social fabric of our nation. The hungry were to be fed. The naked were to be clothed. The homeless were to be sheltered. The jobless were to be employed. The helpless were to be empowered. Racial discrimination was to be eliminated. Women, children, the disabled, and the elderly all were to be given full equality. Through legislation and litigation, through education and communication, through taxation and distribution, the disadvantaged were to be unshackled from the bondage of poverty.[22]

I remember being at home in Appalachia at the time. Folks really believed that a ray of light had burst through to the deep, dark hills of Eastern Kentucky. But that hope was diminished when news spread that much of the "relief" was to be simply given away by the government. Whether these Kentuckians were digging coal from under the flint hills or growing crops on them, they were proud people who were used to working hard for whatever they received. The idea of something for nothing was an anathema to them, and many were never reconciled to the government's giveaways. The stinging loss of a measure of self-respect always accompanied a handout of commodity cheese or butter. They ate it, but they never felt as good about it as they did about what they were able to earn through honest labor.

A funny thing happened on the way to this liberal utopia. Before the "war on poverty," approximately 13 percent of Americans were poor—using the official definition.[23] The unemployment rate was running at less than 4 percent.[24] Over the next forty years, social welfare spending increased more than twenty times, and the welfare bureaucracy grew a hundredfold.[25] The result? Approximately 18 percent of Americans are now poor—again, using the official definition.[26] And the unemployment rate continually fluctuates between 5 percent and 11 percent.[27]

Something has gone wrong—terribly wrong. Forty years and untold billions of dollars later, the hungry are hungrier than ever. The poor, the deprived, the weak, and the dispossessed are more vulnerable than ever. Instead of decreasing the incidence of infant mortality, the "war on poverty" only increased it.[28] Instead of decreasing the incidence of illiteracy, the "war on poverty" only increased it.[29] Instead of decreasing the incidence of unemployment, the "war on poverty" only increased it.[30] We have actually lost ground.[31]

Government programs to help the poor have spawned a number of unintended side effects—unintended, unanticipated, but inevitable—and this despite innumerable efforts to "reform welfare."

First, the implementation of liberal poverty programs and policies has actually halted in its tracks the ongoing improvement in the lot of America's poor. Writers and social scientists from both ends of the ideological spectrum have shown conclusively that instead of enabling the infirm and the elderly to lead full and productive lives, and instead of empowering the poor to control their lives and rise from poverty, social welfare programs have more often than not rendered them impotent, dependent, and helpless.[32] The sheer numbers ought to be enough to convince anyone. After billions upon billions of dollars spent, after a monumental effort that mobilized the ablest minds and the finest machinery, there are more poor than ever before.

There are more homeless than ever before. There are more hungry than ever before. *Something has gone wrong!*

Second, the implementation of liberal poverty programs and policies has actually contributed to the disintegration of poor families.[33] The welfare system subsidizes idleness, provides disincentives to family life, and reduces faith to a blind trust in the protection of the state.[34] Fatherless homes are rewarded with extra benefits and welfare perks, while intact homes are penalized and impoverished. Illegitimate pregnancies are also generously rewarded while moral purity is, likewise, penalized. *Something has gone wrong!*

Third, the implementation of liberal poverty programs and policies has actually provided incentives to avoid work.[35] Each increase in welfare benefits over the past twenty years has resulted in a huge shift from the payrolls to the welfare rolls. When entitlement programs compete with the salaries of lower—or even middle—income families, it is only sensible to expect that many, especially the poorly trained and poorly educated, will choose the path of least resistance. In New York State, for example, a man would have to earn one and a half times the minimum wage to equal the welfare benefits he could receive without working.[36] What inner-city teen is going to work at McDonald's flipping hamburgers for minimum wage when they can "earn" nearly twice that on welfare? *Something has gone wrong!*

Fourth, the implementation of liberal welfare programs and policies has actually contributed to the already enormous problem of governmental waste. Instead of helping to reduce waste by returning more and more citizens to productivity, welfare has proven to be the most inefficient slice of the budgetary pie. Only thirty cents of each antipoverty dollar goes to actual programs to empower the poor or alleviate their plight. And of those thirty cents, only about half ever makes it outside the Washington Beltway.[37] Shocking, but true. All the rest is gobbled up by overhead and administration.

So, during the supposedly "lean and efficient" Reagan years, for example, an average of $124 billion was spent annually to reduce poverty, yet those expenditures reduced poverty by less than $37 billion—not a terribly impressive return on the taxpayers' investment.[38] In theory, the $124 billion should have been enough not only to bring poor households up to the sustenance level, but also to bring these and all other households up to 25 percent above the sustenance level and still have $48 billion left over for other purposes, such as reducing the deficit.[39] *Something has gone wrong!*

Fifth, the implementation of liberal welfare programs and policies has actually reduced the opportunities of the poor in the open marketplace. Walter Williams, in his brilliant book *The State Against Blacks,* and Thomas Sowell, in his equally insightful book *Civil Rights: Rhetoric or Reality?,* have shown beyond any reasonable doubt that most liberal welfare measures decrease work benefits through higher taxes, decrease job creation especially at the lower levels, and decrease entrepreneurial activity due to increased risk.[40] Such measures as the minimum wage, occupational licensing, union supports, and the regulation of the taxi and trucking trades, instead of protecting the unskilled poor, only eliminate them from the marketplace.[41] Upward mobility becomes impossible because the unskilled poor never get to square one. Not only that, everyone else in the economy is harmed as well by the fact that there is less money available for investing. *Something has gone wrong!*

Sixth, the implementation of liberal welfare programs and policies has actually contributed to the demise of American industry. Massive governmental interference in the marketplace has artificially sustained a whole host of antiquated businesses.[42] Instead of launching workers into new fields, new technologies, and new opportunities, welfare's union guarantees, federal bailouts, and job placement programs have encouraged them to remain with stagnating industries, to be content with outdated skills, and to be fearful of innovation. This is one of the reasons that so many of our manufacturing industries have moved overseas. *Something has definitely gone wrong!*

The "war on poverty" has become, in fact, a "war on the poor." Welfare has become a trap, victimizing the very people it was intended to help.

THE CULTURE OF POVERTY AND WELFARE

Lachelle Washington* was just twelve days away from her fifteenth birthday when the test confirmed her suspicions. She was pregnant. And she couldn't have been happier. The way she figured it, her timing was perfect.

Lachelle believed that the pregnancy, far from being an inconvenience, was a ticket to "bigger and better things." Now she would have all the privileges and conveniences that her teenage boyfriends simply could never have hoped to provide.

At least, that was the theory. As a welfare mother, Lachelle assumed that she would have a piece of the "good life." She would be completely out on her own, with no one to answer to and no one to answer for.

It was an opportunity she thought she just couldn't afford to pass up. Like her mother and three older sisters before her, she began to plan her life around her children and the myriad of federal benefits they would be eligible to accrue.

She knew, for instance, that under the government's carefully fabricated system, welfare mothers and their children could actually receive benefits simultaneously from as many as eighteen different programs—covering a dizzying array of family concerns from the basic living expenses of food, shelter, and clothing to health care and child care. Naturally, she applied for them all. And perhaps just as naturally, the legion of social workers and bureaucrats assigned to her case summarily approved her for them all:

- The Child Nutrition Program
- The Food Stamps Program
- The Special Supplemental Food Program
- The Special Milk Program
- The Lower-Income Housing Assistance Program
- The Rent Supplements Program
- The Public Health Services Program

---

*Not her real name

- The Medicaid Program
- The Public Assistance Grants Program
- The Work Incentive Program
- The Employment Services Program
- The Financial Assistance Program for Elementary and Secondary Education
- The Public Assistance Services Program
- The Human Development Services Program
- The Action Domestic Care Program
- The Legal Services Program
- The Community Services Program
- The Head Start Program[43]

Lachelle's situation was hardly unique. Overlap is practically universal among all the hundred-odd welfare assistance programs, since only five of them limit eligibility on the basis of participation in other programs.[44] But even then, when overlap is discovered, recipients are usually not turned away.[45] In fact, many of the programs, including the basic cash subsidy entitlements like Aid for Families with Dependent Children (AFDC), Supplemental Security Income (SSI), social security, and unemployment insurance compensation, actually will encourage applicants to multiply their benefits by applying for any and all overlapping programs.[46]

Lachelle's mother always used to say, "If the government's gonna be givin' it away, we might as well be in on the gettin'." Like mother, like daughter.[47]

But by the time she was twenty-eight, Lachelle had come to the disturbing realization that life on the dole was not all it was cracked up to be. Conditions in the public housing project where she lived were abysmal with persistent violent crime, a rampant drug culture, unsanitary garbage and waste disposal, and hostile neighbors. And despite the fact that all her children had participated in special kindergarten and after-school Head Start programs, she could already see that they were headed down the road to ruin. Her oldest son, Melvin, had acquired a rap sheet longer than his thin, street-toughened arm, and her other three, James, Leslie, and William, were heading in the same direction. None could read or write well enough to fill out even the simplest of forms or applications.

At one point, she had tried to work. But her salary jeopardized her welfare income, and since her earning power was no match for her federal benefits, she quit out of sheer economic necessity. Later, when she'd had a bellyful of welfare, not caring whether she kept her benefits or not, she found that she couldn't keep a job, even a minimum-wage job. She just couldn't adjust to the working life. Welfare had become a trap for her—a dismal, debilitating, disastrous trap.[48]

According to the Children's Defense Fund (CDF)—the major proponent for institutional welfare maintenance today—there is "no evidence" that a "welfare culture" exists in our urban centers.[49] Even though there is overwhelming empirical evidence to the contrary,[50] the CDF and other advocacy and interest groups have unswervingly defended the need for government entitlements. They have become the major obstacle to any form of substantive welfare reform—despite efforts to enact such reform by both sides of the legislative aisle.[51] These groups persistently argue that the experience of second- and third-generation welfare recipients like Lachelle demonstrates the need for more programs, not fewer, for greater spending, not less.[52] They steadfastly deny the apparent failure of the vaunted "war on poverty." "This new myth," they argue, "simply does not accord with logic."[53]

"I don't know much about logic," Lachelle retorts, "but when I look around this neighborhood, I see nothing *but* a welfare culture. It's obvious. It's everywhere. And it's destroying us and what's left of our families. We're enslaved by it—and by the government 'massas' that keep propping it up in the name of justice and compassion."[54]

For Lachelle Washington and millions like her, the "war on poverty" has become a veritable "war on the poor."

A COMPASSION CONSENSUS

Of course, concern for the poor did not begin with Lyndon Johnson and his liberal economic strategists in the sixties. Nor has it been perpetuated by the compassion-industry lobbyists in Washington. In fact, the idea of universal social welfare replaced a long-standing consensus about the role and purpose of government-sponsored relief. It was a consensus that had remained virtually unchanged throughout the history of our nation and, in fact, reached as far back as England's enactment of the Reformation-era Poor Laws.[55]

It was a consensus that operated on the basic admission that civilized societies do not let their people starve in the streets. Instead, they attempt to make some sort of decent provision for those who would otherwise languish helplessly in utter destitution. But that decent provision was by no means a mere handout. It came with limitations, prerequisites, and stipulations. Our forebears were rightly cautious. Though perhaps necessary to the maintenance of civilized societies, government-sponsored emergency relief was still looked upon as a dangerous slippery slope.

Why? Because they believed that the primary responsibility for charity lay with the family, the church, and private institutions—not with the government. Real social security could only be had through the agencies of faith, family, and work.[56] Thus, government welfare was allowed only as a temporary, emergency measure when every other support apparatus failed during times of grave disaster. For centuries this was the unquestioned consensus view of compassion— even among the so-called "ultra-liberals."

Franklin Roosevelt and his New Deal program, for instance, may have radically altered the distribution of welfare with the introduction of social security, AFDC, workman's compensation, and unemployment insurance, but the purposes for social welfare remained unchanged. The consensus remained unchallenged. In 1935, he told Congress, "The federal government must, and shall, quit this business of relief. To dole out relief is to administer a narcotic, a subtle destroyer of the human spirit."[57] Clearly, Roosevelt never intended to create a permanent welfare-disabled underclass.

John Kennedy also held to this view of welfare. In 1962, he launched a poverty assistance offensive with the slogan, "Give a hand, not a handout." The program was based solidly on that old time-tested consensus that no lasting solution to the problem of poverty can be bought with a welfare check. He understood that the best welfare policy is the one that allows the poor to overcome poverty by the only means that have ever proven effectual: by conscientious faith, by a cohesive family, and by disciplined work.

All this was in the grand American tradition. Alexander Hamilton wrote, "Americans hold their greatest liberty in this, our poor arise from their plight of their own accord, in cooperation with, but not dependent upon, Christian generosities."[58] Thomas MacKay wrote, "American welfare consists in a recreation and development of the arts of independence and industry."[59] And Benjamin Franklin was fond of paraphrasing the old Talmudic proverb, asserting that American charity "is the noblest charity, preventing a man from accepting charity, and the best alms, enabling men to dispense with alms."[60] So America came to be known the world over as the home of the free and the brave, the land of opportunity.

That old consensus died in 1964. It was the first casualty in the "war on poverty."

The members of President Lyndon Johnson's task force on poverty—including Michael Harrington, author of the influential book *The Other America*; Bill Moyers, the high-profile telejournalist; Sargent Shriver, pioneer of the Peace Corps; and Joseph Califano, later a chief aide to President Jimmy Carter—forged a new and invincible consensus.

This new consensus decried the old consensus as "harsh," "unrealistic," "insensitive," and "discriminatory." Rejecting the notion that poverty was in any way connected with individual or family irresponsibility, the new consensus adamantly asserted that poverty was the fault of the system. Environment was the problem. Oppression, discrimination, materialism, and injustice were the main causes. And society was to blame.[61] Thus, society would have to pay.[62]

One day, Califano called a group of reporters, social workers, and activists into his office at the White House to explain the president's plan to increase social welfare spending. He told them that a government analysis had shown that only fifty thousand people, or about 1 percent of the eight million people on permanent welfare, were capable of being trained to make themselves self-sufficient. Of the other twelve million people on temporary welfare programs, only about half were trainable, he said.[64]

In other words, the architects of the welfare system assumed that there was already a hopelessly untrainable underclass. Rather than transform poverty, they set out to institutionalize it. A modern form of governmental slavery was thus created—and all in the name of compassion. The American Dream had been transformed into what Star Parker has called "Uncle Sam's Plantation."

True Compassion

What then should compassionate American taxpayers and voters actually be advocating? What can the government do to reverse its dismal welfare track record? What can the government do to *really* help the poor?

Perhaps the best answer is, "Get out of the way." As economist Murray Rothbard has argued:

> Let the government get out of the way of the productive energies of all groups in the population—rich, middle-class, and poor alike—and the result will be an enormous increase in the welfare and the standard of living of everyone, and most particularly of the poor who are the ones supposedly helped by the miscalled welfare state.[64]

If the government were to reduce the level of taxation, remove industrial restraints, eliminate wage controls, and abolish subsidies, tariffs, and other constraints on free enterprise, the poor would be helped in a way that AFDC, social security, and unemployment insurance could never match. Jobs would be created, investment would be stimulated, productivity would soar, and technology would advance. If that were to happen, argued Rothbard, "the lower income groups would benefit *more* than anyone else."[65]

The "war on the poor" can be turned around. It can be as it was intended to be from the start: a "war on poverty." But only if the government leaves the "war" machinery substantially alone. But only if the government leaves the "war" machinery substantially to *us*.[66]

Like honoring our parents, caring for the poor is a command with a promise. The Bible tells us that if we would uphold the mandate to be generous to the poor, we would ourselves be happy (Prov. 14:21), God would preserve us (Ps. 41:1–2), we would prosper and be satisfied (Prov. 11:25), and we would be raised up from beds of affliction (Ps. 41:3). All throughout the Scriptures, Christians are reminded that care for the needy is at the heart of true faith.[67] Thus it has always been the aspiration of faithful churches to be "zealous for good works" (Titus 2:14).

When I was young, I heard a saying back home in eastern Kentucky that went like this: "It's like pounding sand down a rat hole." I asked my father what it meant. He said it was the essence of futility, of undertaking a hopeless task.

Ronald Reagan made the statement, "The liberals fought poverty, and poverty won." Why, after forty years of government programs and billions of dollars of tax money, do we still have the same problems we had before the so-called "war on poverty" began?

The liberal agenda has created a permanent underclass with programs that promise freedom and produce slavery. Immorality is rewarded, and the only way to increase personal income is to produce more illegitimate children. The best way for a father to help his family financially is by abandoning them so they can receive the resources of the welfare state.

Could it be because the government has been trying to do things that others should be doing? Could it be that we can never legislate or formulate bureaucratic answers to questions that can only find their appropriate responses from individuals and organizations that know how to help people from the inside out, instead of from the outside in? Have our billions of dollars been only so much sand pounded down the proverbial rat hole?

Charles Haddon Spurgeon, the great Victorian social reformer and pastor, said, "They say you may praise a fool till you make him useful: I don't know much about that, but I do know that if I get a bad knife I generally cut my finger, and a blunt axe is far more trouble than profit. A handsaw is a good thing—but not to shave with. A pig's tail will never make a good arrow; nor will his ear make a silk purse. You can't catch rabbits with drums or pigeons with plums. A good thing is not good out of its place."[68]

I'm willing to consider the fact that the architects of the modern welfare system intended to do good. Certainly their motivation to help the poorest of the poor is commendable. Yet, as Spurgeon says, a good thing is not a good thing out of its place. Ronald Reagan was absolutely right: the war on poverty was won by poverty. This is because the churches in America abandoned their proper role in society. We were silent when we should have been speaking. We were inactive when we should have been proactive.

The problem with modern agendas to care for the poor is not that the legion of welfare activists wants to do a good thing. It is that a good thing is not good out of its place. As Wall Street journalist Gerald Wisz has argued, "Government cannot do what the church must."[69]

Action Points

- Visit www.compassionbycommand.com for information on the Compassion by Command program, which is a seven-week course enabling churches to reach out to the poor.

- Implement S.A.Y. Yes! Youth Centers in your area. This program provides a biblically based curriculum in an after-school program that teaches Bible study, computer training, mentoring, and more. Visit www.sayyescenters.org for more information.

- Holistic Hardware is a program that teaches church workers how to help those who are living in poverty build a spiritual and practical foundation to help them help themselves. Visit www.holistichardware.com to start this program in your church.

- Find out information on Faith-Based Initiatives and Community Initiatives at www.whitehouse .gov/government/fbci.

- Volunteer at a local food bank or homeless shelter.

- Advocate government policies that link compassion and responsibility, and that place value on keeping families together.

- Learn more about poverty and how you can get involved in the fight against poverty on a personal and national level with the Coalition on Urban Renewal and Education (CURE). Visit their Web site at www.urbancure.org.

CHAPTER 4

HOMOSEXUALITY:
The Unhappy Gay Agenda
SILENT NO MORE

> Purity is the beginning of all passion. Thus, faithful
> marriage is the only guarantee of unbridled sexual
> pleasure.
>
> —HENRY WADSWORTH LONGFELLOW

The character of American society and life is being sorely tested by an astonishing trend in the homosexual community. It is a trend that could very well completely transform our culture.

Couples are getting married in surprising numbers.

But it's not what you think. It's not what the newsmakers, commentators, and politicians have been bantering about during the past year or so. It's not what anyone expected. Indeed, it is a trend that hardly anyone has even noticed yet. But it is one of the most significant societal shifts in recent memory.

Now to be sure, *gay marriage* is a hot topic these days. It may have received more attention during the 2004 election season than any other social debate in history. It even may have been the deciding factor in the presidential race. At the end of the evening, all eyes were on Ohio, one of the eleven states that had marriage amendments on the ballots. Along with others who believed in moral standards, I gave my best effort in educating people in my home state about the dangers of being silent while others who opposed traditional marriage trumpeted their point of view by every outlet available to them. Would evangelicals and others who had traditional values show up to defend marriage? Thankfully, they did—but how many of them would not have had sufficient motivation without the same-sex marriage issue?

In November 2003, Massachusetts removed the final obstacle in becoming the first state in the country to legalize homosexual unions after the state's highest court struck down a ban on same-sex marriages. The 4-3 ruling, which stopped short of declaring that homosexual couples should be granted marriage licenses, mirrored a 1999 decision by the neighboring Vermont Supreme Court, which also put the question of legalization into the hands of state lawmakers. Both landmark decisions gave homosexual advocates another foothold in the burgeoning national debate over legalizing same-sex unions. They lent further support to the watershed U.S. Supreme Court ruling in June 2003 in which justices rejected a longtime ban on same-sex sodomy in Texas. That case was widely viewed as the "*Roe v. Wade*" for homosexual activists.

Early in 2004, when the state of Massachusetts quickly followed the city of San Francisco in issuing marriage licenses for lesbian, gay, transsexual, bisexual, and transgender couples, the majority of Americans looked on in shock and dismay. And with concurring court decisions in Hawaii, New York, and throughout Canada, and with cases pending in nineteen other states, it has begun to appear as if a genuine sea change in the legal environment is occurring before our very eyes.

But the court decisions, the legislative initiatives, the bureaucratic maneuvers, and all the hand-wringing that they have elicited among family advocates across America have little or nothing to do with the remarkable resurgence of marriage sweeping through the homosexual communities. That is because the surprising marital trend that offers a new test of American character is not the legalization of these same-sex unions. Instead, it is the trend in the gay community toward the old-fashioned, bride and groom, husband and wife, male and female kind of marriages.

Yes, that's right: men and women. And they are not marriages of convenience or efforts to skirt adoption or child-custody regulations. These are for-real marriages. You know, the "to have and to hold, for richer, for poorer, in sickness and in health, to love and to cherish, until death do us part" sort of marriages.

According to Bob Hertzmann, "This is not exactly the sort of thing the TV networks are likely to tell folks about." In fact, he asserts that this remarkable new trend may very well be "the most under-reported story in America right now."[1] And he should know. Hertz-mann is a local counseling coordinator for Exodus International, an organization that has helped hundreds of gay men and women abandon their homosexual practices over the last several years while finding fulfillment, satisfaction, and freedom in welcoming churches, in healthy relationships, and in monogamous marriages.

Hertzmann and his wife, Lisa, are living examples of this trend. "I was an activist in New York for the radical homosexual advocacy group ACT UP. Lisa was a practicing lesbian involved with a local AIDS support agency. We met at several political rallies through the years. But both of us were so enmeshed in our own worlds, our own troubles, and our own relationships that we never even really paid much attention to each other. But then we both happened to meet at a Bible study. I was shocked to see her. She was shocked to see me. It turns out though, that like so many gays, we were both terribly sad, and we were both beginning to search for something more."[2]

Over the next several months, the two of them explored the claims of Christianity. "We were amazed to discover that the hunger for significance we'd both always had was satisfied, not only in the Christian faith, but in the Christian community. As our hearts began to heal from many years of abuse, promiscuity, and desperation, we began to feel again for the first time in a very long time. And then it just happened; to our extraordinary surprise, we fell in love. The rest, as they say, is history."[3]

Amazingly, Bob and Lisa's love story is becoming more and more common in the homosexual community. John Thompson, a clinical psychologist practicing in Buffalo, New York, has said, "As men and women become more and more disillusioned with the gay lifestyle, they look for alternatives, answers, anything. In desperation, they turn to local churches or ministries like Exodus International, Harvest Ministries, or Homosexuals Anonymous. There they encounter dozens of others who once were bound by sexual addictions and other compulsive behaviors—who are now free, happy, and hopeful for the future. For them, it is a stunning revelation."[4]

Of course, the current popular myth is that homosexuals are born with their same-sex attractions. It argues that they cannot change. It asserts that their sexual orientation is determined biologically. "I am living proof that such politically correct maxims are just not true," says Hertzmann. "And there are hundreds, even thousands of others just like me. The proof is in the pudding."

It appears that he is not exaggerating at all. If the testimonies on the Exodus International Web site or the documentary evidence compiled by Focus on the Family is any indication, the number of former homosexuals, transsexuals, bisexuals, and lesbians who have left their promiscuous lifestyles to embrace traditional values, the Christian faith, and ordinary family life is increasing every day. Support groups are springing up in virtually every major city across the country. Newsletters, magazines, journals, books, tapes, and films now abound. And wedding bells are ringing. As author, lecturer, and former homosexual Joe McCallum has said, "The homosexual community now has a back door as wide as the broadside of a barn—and people are pouring through it into the church and into healthy families."[5]

Any number of politicians, media pundits, and cultural critics are scrambling to deal with the issue of same-sex marriages in a fashion that somehow will not undermine inheritance, property, and insurance laws while at the same time satisfying the demands of the homosexual lobbyists and activists. Meanwhile, this dramatic new trend within the homosexual community may well be making such efforts unnecessary. "The best way to deal with a difficult problem is not always to attack the problem itself but to focus on the solution," Michael Spinnaker, another counselor for Exodus, has said. "The sudden spate of marriages we're seeing among former homosexuals is only surprising because the media has steadfastly avoided reporting the story. But it is one of the most amazing and wonderful stories to be told. And it makes the hubbub over same-sex unions pale in comparison."[6]

Of course, the obvious question is, "Why?" Why are gays turning away from the homosexual life and culture in record numbers? Why is their much-lauded "alternative lifestyle" becoming increasingly unattractive to the very people who ought to be most committed to it? Why is it that the greatest danger to the continued expansion of "gay rights" is now coming not from the "Religious Right" or the "conservative moralists" but from the "inside hardcore?"

PROFOUNDLY UNHAPPY

There is no use denying the fact that many gays aren't truly gay at all. Remember, the original definition of the word *gay* had no homosexual orientation. Instead, it was a word that meant to "to be happy and carefree." Homosexuals are anything but happy and carefree. In fact, indications are that they are a very sad lot indeed. According to virtually every scientific, medical, and sociological study of the homosexual community, the everyday world of the American homosexual is a very unhappy world.

For instance, a study published in a recent issue of the prestigious *American Journal of Public Health* found that more than 21 percent of all gays had made suicide plans at one time or another, and 12 percent had actually made attempts on their own lives at least once.[7] Those are staggering statistics.

In another study of the effect of homosexuality on public health and social order, researchers found that gays had "substantially higher participation in sadomasochism, fisting, bestiality, ingestion of feces, orgies, large numbers of sexual partners, deliberate infection of others, cheating in marriage, obscene phone calls, criminality, shoplifting, and tax cheating."[8] Hardly the stuff of *Queer Eye for the Straight Guy*.

Other researchers found gays suffered from extraordinarily low self-esteem and disproportionately high rates of depression, leading them to submit themselves to humiliatingly passive roles in their relationships. Indeed, they found that nearly 88 percent submitted themselves to submissive and masochistic sexual bondage roles.[9]

And it is not just the emotional health of gays that suffers. Given that their sexual practices and lifestyle choices make health and hygiene a practical impossibility, ill health is an inescapable part of the gay lifestyle.

Besides the fact that gay socializing revolves around the bar scene—with its incumbent drinking, drugs, and late-night carousing— gay sexuality inevitably involves brutal physical abusiveness and the unnatural imposition of alien substances into internal organs, orally and anally, that inevitably suppress the immune system and heighten susceptibility to disease.[10] In fact, gay sex is a veritable breeding ground of disease.[11] Among them are colonitis, an excruciating inflammation of the mucus membrane; mucosal ulcers in the rectum; and Kobner's phenomenon, a psoriasis of the rectum and genitals.[12] In addition, a group of rare bowel diseases, previously considered tropical, are now epidemic in urban gay communities. Popularly dubbed "Gay Bowel Syndrome," these afflictions include: amebiasis, a colon disease caused by parasites that produce abscesses, ulcers, and diarrhea;[13] giardiasis, a parasitic bowel disease, again causing diarrhea and sometimes enteritis;[14] shigellosis, a bacterial bowel disease causing severe dysentery;[15] and hepatitis A, a viral liver disease, which its victims can spread to others through handling food and even through the water splashed on toilet seats.[16]

Even the more conventional sexually transmitted diseases are especially acute among homosexuals. Male homosexuals are actually fourteen times more likely to have had syphilis than heterosexuals, eight times more likely to have had hepatitis A or B, and hundreds of times more likely to have had oral infection by venereal diseases through penile contact.[17] Furthermore, female homosexuals are nineteen times more likely to have had syphilis than their heterosexual counterparts, twice as likely to have had genital warts, four times as likely to have had scabies, seven times more likely to have had infection from vaginal contact, twenty-nine times more likely to have had oral infection from vaginal contact, and twelve times more likely to have had an oral infection from penile contact than female heterosexuals.[18]

And then there is AIDS.

Dr. Luc Montagnier of Paris' Pasteur Institute, who first isolated what is now called the human immunodeficiency virus (HIV), which is generally supposed to be the retroviral cause of AIDS, has argued that promiscuity among homosexuals may have created the disease in the first place. *Time* magazine revealed that "Montagnier supported a controversial theory that Mycoplasma, a bacterium-like organism, is the trigger that turns a slow-growing population of AIDS viruses into mass killers. According to Montagnier, the explosion of sexual activity during the 1970s fostered the spread of a hardy drug-resistant strain of Mycoplasma. HIV, meanwhile, lay dormant in Africa. The AIDS epidemic began, Montagnier speculates, when the two microbes got together, perhaps in Haiti."[19]

Despite such overwhelming medical evidence, for years homosexuals ignored health warnings and for the most part still engaged in dangerous behaviors. A study of 655 homosexual men in San Francisco found that while "knowledge of health guidelines was quite high, this knowledge actually had no relation to sexual behavior."[20]

In fact, the idea that homosexuals should limit their promiscuous encounters seemed to be entirely untenable to homosexuals. During the first International Conference on AIDS, for instance, researchers

75

concluded that simply being informed about the AIDS virus does not make people any more likely to practice safe sex.[21]

Amazingly, even the experts themselves were undeterred from practicing promiscuous behavior. As renowned gay historian Frank Browning reported, "Any residual doubts about the place of sex— hot, sweaty, raunchy sex—in the AIDS-prevention campaign disappeared at the global conference on AIDS in Montreal. For five days the discos were packed with gay doctors, nurses, activists, and researchers shamelessly cruising one another. A nearby bathhouse was doing a land-office business. A [gay sex] club posted promotional fliers in the conference exhibit hall. And in the middle of the hall a monitor was showing a 'safe sex' video sponsored by a West German health agency. The video was played and replayed all day long for two days, and there seemed never to be fewer than twenty-five or thirty viewers—men, women, straight, gay—gathered about the screen in a fidgety semicircle. Two men who, except for their blondeness, might have been Michelangelo's models were demonstrating a wide array of 'safe' erotic possibilities."[22]

It should not be surprising, therefore, that the life expectancy of gays is substantially lower than that of heterosexuals, according to hosts of new studies. One Canadian study found that 95 percent of extant HIV-AIDS cases were distributed among gay and bisexual men.[23] Nearly all the rest were among intravenous drug users. As a result, age-specific mortality was significantly higher for gay and bisexual men than for all other demographic categories.[24] Even without AIDS, the homosexual community is sick and dying. The median age of homosexual men dying from AIDS is thirty-nine.[25] The median age of homosexual men dying from all other causes is forty-two.[26] The median age of lesbians at death is forty-five.[27] Compared with the population at large—where the median age at death for men is seventy-five and for women is seventy-nine—those are sobering figures.[28] Only 1 percent of homosexuals die of old age.[29] Less than 3 percent of all homosexuals today are over the age of fifty-five.[30] In fact, researchers found that the best gays could hope for was a life expectancy comparable to that for males living in 1871.[31] Amazing! Homosexual practice has practically abrogated all the medical advances of the twentieth century!

And that is not all. Even without taking into account the extraordinarily high morbidity rate, the numbers of gays in the population have been grossly overexaggerated through the years. The now discredited *Kinsey Report* asserted that more than 10 percent of the American population was homosexual.[32] For years the media and even the scientific community accepted that statistic. But recent studies have shown that the actual number is closer to 2 or 3 percent. The most recent National Health and Social Life Survey conducted by researchers at the University of Chicago found the homosexual rate among women was just over 1 percent, and among men it was just over 2.5 percent.[33] Thus, gays are not only sad; they are lonely.

Despite the fact that homosexuals tend to be better educated and have higher per capita incomes than the general population, those advantages are not translated into happiness. Researchers uncovered the disturbing fact that gays turn toward drugs and alcohol in disproportionate numbers in an effort to ease their pains and drown their sorrows. According to one study, "Substantially higher proportions of the homosexual sample used alcohol, marijuana, or cocaine than was the case in the general population."[34]

"Looking back," Bob Hertzmann has said, "I now realize that I never knew a happy, contented, well-adjusted, and healthy homosexual. In all my years enmeshed in the gay lifestyle, I never met anyone who actually was gay."[35]

Hopping Mad

These dismal facts help to explain why people like Bob and Lisa Hertzmann are abandoning the gay world in increasing numbers. But they also help to explain why those who remain committed to their unhappy and unhealthy lifestyles are becoming more and more radical, more and more brazen, and more and more desperate.

This was all too evident a few years ago when the members of a small Baptist church in San Francisco gathered for Sunday evening worship. A guest speaker had been invited to address the congregation on the subject of homosexuality. Although there had been no public notice of the special event—just a brief mention in the church's regular Sunday bulletin—a local homosexual tabloid announced the meeting with a splashy front-page spread.

According to the pastor, David Innes, that week the church received a number of threatening phone calls. "They demanded that our guest not be allowed to speak—and they said that they intended to stop him if he tried."

Fearful that there might be some kind of an altercation, the pastor placed several calls to the San Francisco police. He was reassured that he and his congregation would be completely safe.

About an hour before the service was scheduled to begin, dozens of belligerent homosexual demonstrators began gathering around the church facilities. They carried signs and banners bearing messages like "We're Here and We're Queer," "Refuse and Resist," "Queens, Queers, and Quays," "Bash Back," "Dykes on Bykes," "Dykes with Tykes," "I'm a Lesbian…Get Used to It," and other curse-laden phrases. Threatening lethal violence, they blocked entryways and crowded onto sidewalks and adjacent properties.

Before long a full-scale riot was underway. The little church building was vandalized. Frightened members of the congregation were surrounded and harassed as they arrived in the parking lot. One woman was accosted and nearly dragged out of the frantic clutches of her family. Rocks and eggs pelted the doors and windows of the sanctuary.

Blocking traffic of two busy thoroughfares, several protesters began to shout obscenities and shriek perverse slogans over megaphones and portable sound systems. Along the side of the church building several more pounded fiercely on the walls, windows, and doors. Others exposed themselves to passersby and simulated sex acts with one another. A fluttering lavender and pink flag was run up the flagpole, and lurid posters were plastered throughout the property.

Inside the besieged church, children clung to their parents in terror. One elderly blind woman—mistaking the pounding and banging for gunshots—became hysterical. Attempting to maintain some semblance of order, Innes assured the congregation that the police would protect them.

In fact, the police seemed either helpless to come to the aid of the church members, or they deliberately chose not to. Although Innes and others repeatedly requested that the officers call for backup, none was forthcoming. And no arrests were made.

When the church members finally decided to try to leave for their homes, the rioters surged toward the building with new fury. In an eerie replay of the scene at Sodom, several began to chant, "We want your children. Give us your children."

Several hours after it had begun, the melee slowly dissipated. But before leaving the property, the last of the rioters promised, "We will be back. This war is not over. It has just begun."[36]

THE RADICALIZATION OF THE MOVEMENT

This incident in San Francisco is just one example of the radicalization of the unhappy gay movement. But we need not rely on anecdotal evidence to prove that notion. The fact is, the homosexual world is rife with revolutionary rhetoric—and it has carefully mobilized itself to translate that rhetoric into action. Ready or not, here they come. The radical agenda of these few activists is all too open and obvious.

Writing in *The Advocate*, the nation's most prestigious homosexual magazine, radical gay apologist Steve Warren asserted:

> Now the tide has turned. We have at last "come out,"
> and in so doing we have exposed the mean-spirited
> nature of Judeo-Christian morality. You have been
> narrow-minded and self-righteous. But with the
> help of a growing number of your own membership,

we are going to force you to recant everything you have believed or said about sexuality.[37]

Warren went on to offer a startling list of the movement's non-negotiable demands:

Here are some of the things you will be expected to affirm in the process of renouncing love, marriage and family:

1. Henceforth, homosexuality will be spoken of in your churches and synagogues as an "honorable estate."

2. You can either let us marry people of the same sex, or better yet, abolish marriage altogether, since it will give the lie to everything you have said or done about sexuality.

3. ...You will also instruct your young people in homosexual as well as heterosexual behavior, and you will go out of your way to make certain that homosexual youths are allowed to date, attend religious functions together, openly display affection, and enjoy each other's sexuality without embarrassment or guilt.

4. If any of the older people in your midst object, you will deal with them sternly, making certain they renounce their ugly and ignorant homophobia or suffer public humiliation.

5. You will also make certain that all of the prestige and resources of your institutions are brought to bear on the community, so that laws are passed forbidding discrimination against homosexuals and heavy punishments are assessed.

6. Finally, we will in all likelihood want to expunge a number of passages from your Scriptures and rewrite others, eliminating preferential treatment of marriage and using words that will allow for homosexual interpretations of passages.[38]

Warren then concluded with this warning:

If all these things do not come to pass quickly, we will subject Orthodox Jews and Christians to the most sustained hatred and vilification in recent memory. We have captured the liberal establishment and the press. We have already beaten you on a number of battlefields. And we have the spirit of the age on our side. You have neither the faith nor the strength to fight us, so you might as well surrender now.[39]

This is no bluff. This is the profile of the new "political correctness." This is the radical face of "cultural diversity," "tolerance," and "inclusiveness."

The justification for such drastic demands, of course, is the "ever-escalating" problem of "gay-bashing"—the supposedly commonplace violence committed against homosexuals by heterosexual bigots. The media trumpets such claims—that homosexuals are continually assaulted by "homophobes" who are no doubt inspired by Christian or right-wing prejudices.[40] In fact, according to recent FBI hate crime statistics, out of the more than thirteen million annual criminal offenses, only about eight thousand are hate crimes. Sixty percent of those eight thousand are motivated by racial conflicts, 17 percent are motivated by religious prejudice, and only 13 percent are motivated by sexual orientation.[41] While these few antigay "hate crimes" are often highlighted, the media seems to have somehow overlooked any and all acts of violence committed by homosexuals against straight families and institutions.

The hundreds of such incidents reported each year cover the gamut from vandalism to rape, from assault to institutional blackmail.[42] And law enforcement officials estimate that straight-bashing incidents may be under-reported by as much as 70 percent.[43]

Threats, intimidation, and violence against the Christian community in particular are an increasingly evident problem.[44] When an ordinance was placed on the ballot in Oregon that would have prohibited the government from endorsing or recognizing homosexuality as a legitimate alternate lifestyle, flyers suddenly appeared on telephone poles *warning* people to vote against it. One showed the Christian *icthus* fish being roasted on a stick over fire. It read, "YOU BURN US, WE BURN YOU." Another flyer showed the same *icthus* and warned Christians to vote against the ordinance "OR WE SHOOT THE FISH." Another said, "CIVIL RIGHTS or CIVIL WAR. Your choice for a limited time only."

And it is not just Christian politicians or civil activists that the straight-bashers target. For years Dan Doell of Kansas City spent his time caring for AIDS patients at the Samuel Rodgers Community Health Clinic. Yet, despite his selfless work on behalf of homosexuals, he has been denounced as a traitor and a "missionary of hate" by various radical homosexual groups.[45]

Doell's offense? It was simply that he—like so many others—had the audacity to repent of homosexuality. After being seduced as a teenager, Doell spent ten years of his life as a practicing homosexual before leaving the lifestyle. Now he speaks to various groups in an effort to expose how arbitrary it is to base one's identity on one's sexual proclivities. As he often asserts, "People don't stand on a street corner or wear a T-shirt that says, 'I'm greedy,' or 'I'm a gossiper. I was born that way, and I'll never change.'"[46]

For his apostasy from the homosexual subculture, gay activists in Kansas City started a letter-writing campaign to get Doell fired from his job caring for sick and dying homosexuals. While they attempt to make sure no one can fire them for their own sexual practices, homosexuals seem all too ready to use intimidation to get others fired.

John Freeman, the executive director of Harvest Ministry in Philadelphia, is another repentant former homosexual. His ministry has had great success in ministering to homosexuals and discipling them into a moral lifestyle. According to *World* magazine, "People who follow the 'once gay always gay' belief usually do not look at the choices in life, Freeman said. People are rarely consciously aware of when they started feeling same-sex attractions, but when actions are traced through the years, small choices began to accumulate."[47]

Claiming that homosexuality involves choice causes fury among homosexual activists. The offices of Harvest have received numerous bomb threats. The staff has also received other hysterically hostile phone calls. In one incident, sixty demonstrators tried to force their way into the building and take over the offices. But for some odd reason, this doesn't count as a hate crime.[48]

MAKING THE WORLD SAFE FOR DEBAUCHERY

The pressure on society to accept the audacious behaviors and disastrous consequences of homosexual activity is not a matter of cultural drift or shifting mores. It is a carefully orchestrated, highly organized, and extremely disciplined political program. And it is a program that has achieved extraordinary success in recent years.

When Bill Clinton first ran for president, he made a bold and brash pledge to homosexual activists at a fund-raiser in Los Angeles. "I have a vision," he said, "and you're part of it."[49]

That pledge ultimately proved to be his best-kept campaign promise. The president's controversial push to open the U.S. military to admitted homosexuals was just the tip of the iceberg.[50] Even though he quickly reneged on key campaign pledges made to much larger, mainstream constituencies, early on the president took steps to make good on his commitment to the gay political agenda.

Besides instituting his sweeping "Don't Ask, Don't Tell" directive, which effectively lifted the ban on gays in the military, the president ordered a whole series of administrative policy changes—unleashing a veritable tidal wave of government-promoted homosexual advocacy that endures to the present day.

For instance, the Office of Personnel Management issued formal recognition to a homosexual employees group within the federal bureaucracy, saying any future questions about homosexuality in background checks of applicants or employees would be prohibited.[51] The White House revised its Equal Employment Opportunity Statement and bestowed "protected minority class" status on homosexuals working there.[52] Attorney General Janet Reno issued an order to all branches of the Justice Department—including the FBI—that forbade discrimination based on sexual orientation, status, or conduct.[53]

In addition to these measures, Clinton made dozens of specific promises to the homosexual movement that ultimately helped to dramatically reshape federal priorities, including the implementation of affirmative action policies for homosexuals;[54] the lifting of content restrictions for the National Endowment for the Arts, the Public Broadcasting Service, and National Public Radio;[55] and the appointment of hundreds of new judges, administrators, and bureaucrats committed to the gay agenda. Indeed, during the early days of his administration, he bragged to the *Washington Blade*, a homosexual tabloid in the nation's capital, that he had appointed more than two dozen homosexuals to high-level positions in the administration and hundreds more throughout the federal bureaucracy.[56]

"We conquered the world," said Larry Kramer, ACT UP's founder and leading light.[57] Although that is probably a bit of an exaggeration, without a doubt, the Clinton administration legitimized and institutionalized the gay lobby. Clearly, stronger than ever before, with more influence and more opportunities than ever before, the gay movement had come of age. Today, every government agency at every level is now receptive to the demands of homosexual activists, regardless of how those demands may compromise the health, security, or welfare of the general population.

Al Gore based many of his campaign promises on the solid pro-homosexual stance of the Clinton administration. And when John Kerry launched his own campaign for president, his Web site touted him as the "most pro-gay presidential candidate ever." Kerry's campaign announced a "Pride Across America" program targeting the homosexual community with booths at sixty "Gay Pride" events in twenty-two states during the course of the campaign. Available were "Out for Kerry 2004" buttons and flyers as well as a "LBGT for John Kerry" Web site featuring a "Kerry Pride Guide," with a "Kerry Pride Toolkit" that included postcards, flyers, and sign-up sheets. Kerry scored a "100 percent" rating from the Human Rights Campaign, a leading homosexual advocacy group, when he opposed a constitutional amendment affirming traditional marriage and when he supported Vermont-style civil unions for "Gays, Lesbians, Bis, and Transgenders."[58] Senator Kerry's wife, Teresa Heinz-Kerry, reportedly pledged "...to make gay tolerance a centerpiece of her First Lady duties," according to one media source.[59]

The gay agenda has not only made it into the political mainstream; it *is* the political mainstream. And the liberal media is making sure we hear no end of it all. In 1998 Matthew Shepherd, a homosexual, was beaten unconscious and left to die in Wyoming. The crime garnered national and even international media attention. More than 3,007 news stories were generated in the U.S. alone. I'm sure you remember the case.

But at about the same time there was another case. For some reason the heinous murder of Jesse Durkhising did not make the headlines. Why? Because thirteen-year-old Jesse was raped by two homosexuals before he was brutally killed. Across the nation, there were forty-six stories about Jesse. According to Andrew Sullivan, an openly homosexual columnist for the *New Republic*, the Shepherd case was hyped for political reasons to build support for the inclusion of homosexuals in a federal hate crimes law. And the Durkhising case was ignored for the same political reasons. As Sullivan, himself openly gay, asserted, "Some deaths, if they affect a politically protected class, are worth more than those who don't."[60]

No wonder the homosexual movement seems to be winning the culture war at every turn. "Who would have ever dreamed that we would be in this kind of a position—even just a few years ago?" exulted Bryce Tomlinson.[61] "We're basically in the driver's seat politically and culturally. To change the metaphor, the deck is stacked entirely in our favor." Tomlinson, an ACT UP coordinator in Maryland, was hardly bragging when he asserted, "We've made the difference. We're here, we're queer, and we're in charge. Get used to it."[62]

LEGISLATING MORALITY

Apologists for the gay agenda have argued that the only reason they have had to resort to extreme activism is that traditional values oppress not only the homosexual community but also everyone. They argue that to impose "community standards" of ethics and decency is "a violation of the spirit of American democracy" and a "contradiction of our most basic constitutional tenants."[63] Thus, any attempt to do so goes beyond "bigotry" or "intolerance" to "despotism" and "tyranny."[64]

You simply "can't legislate morality," they say. One social commentator, after rehearsing a long litany of the fleshly excesses of elected officials in Washington, followed that up by saying, "...as Congress ought to know."

On the contrary, as Dr. D. James Kennedy has so often asserted, "morality is the only thing you *can* legislate."[65] That's what legislation *is*. It is the codification in law of some particular moral concern—generally so that the immorality of a few is not forcibly inflicted on the rest of us.[66]

Murder is against the law because we recognize that the premeditated killing of another human being is a violation of a very basic and fundamental moral principle—a moral principle that we all hold dear: the sanctity of human life. Theft is against the law because we recognize that taking someone else's belongings without permission is a breach of another one of our most basic and fundamental ethical standards: private property. The fact is, all law is some moral or ethical idea enforced by the civil government.

Thus, the question is not, "Should we legislate morality?" Rather, it is, "Whose morality should we legislate?" The question is, "What moral standard will we use when we legislate?"

In the Western world, it appears that we are legislating immorality more than anything else. Ake Green, a pastor from Sweden, was recently sentenced to one month in prison for inciting hatred against homosexuals. Green was prosecuted for a sermon he preached, citing biblical references to homosexuality, in which he described homosexuality as "abnormal, a horrible cancerous tumor in the body of society." The prosecutor in the case justified the arrest of Pastor Green: "One may have whatever religion one wishes, but this is an attack on all fronts against homosexuals. Collecting Bible citations on this topic as he does makes this hate speech."[67]

Pastor Green is not alone. Magistrates have threatened Canadian Christians, French teachers, Dutch businessmen, and even American soccer moms with prosecution for daring to say what the Bible says, what the entire culture once knew to be true: homosexuality is not just sick; it is sin.

California State Senator Sheila Kuehl sponsored Senate Bill 1234, later signed into law, which was modeled after Canadian legislation that makes it illegal to speak against homosexuals in that country. In Canada, a publisher and newspaper have recently been prosecuted for printing an ad that contained scriptures referencing homosexuality. The intent of SB 1234 is to redefine what constitutes a "hate crime" in California. Under this legislation, individuals could claim that someone expressing their deeply held beliefs, whether political or religious, presents an "intimidating" threat that is punishable by law. Penalties for violating SB 1234 include criminal prosecution and fines of $25,000. The fine is awarded to the one who brings the accusation. The effect of a bill like this would be to censor all Californians from their constitutional right of free speech when articulating what the Bible states regarding the sinful nature of homosexuality.

Welcome to the brave new world of political correctness run amok.

At this critical juncture in American history and life, we are facing an extraordinary test of character. Will we bend the knee to the gods of political correctness? Will we lend credence to the unhappy prophets of the homosexual agenda? Or will we pay heed to the legions of men and women like Bob and Lisa Hertzmann—men and women who have found their way out of bondage and into freedom and opportunity?

ACTION POINTS

- Visit www.exodusglobalalliance.org for helpful information about coming out of the homosexual lifestyle.

- Push for passage of the Marriage Protection Amendment to the United States Constitution.

- Identify and avoid popular culture outlets (television programs, movies, etc.) that glorify ungodly lifestyles.

- Apply pressure to local media outlets to stop the obvious bias toward homosexuality.

- Visit www.protectmarriage.org to find out about the status of pending pro-marriage legislation.

- Recommended reading:
  Getting It Straight, by Peter Sprigg and Timothy J. Dailey, eds., which gives the truth about homosexuality and identifies the half-truths and myths surrounding it[68]

CHAPTER 5

ISLAM:
The Deception of Allah
SILENT NO MORE

> Allah, there is no strength but your strength. Destroy, therefore, the Zionist occupation and its helpers and its agents. Destroy the U.S. and its helpers and its agents. Destroy Britain and its helpers and its agents. Prepare those who will soon unite the Muslims of the world and march in the footsteps of Saladin. Allah, we ask you for forgiveness, forgiveness before death, and mercy and forgiveness after death. Allah, grant victory to Islam and the Muslims in the coming war.
>
> —THE PRAYER OF THE MUFTI OF
> JERUSALEM, SHEIKH EKRIMA SOBRI,
> TWO WEEKS BEFORE SEPTEMBER 11, 2001

I am not a spiritual person. I am actually a little suspicious of those who are. I have met too many granola people (fruits, flakes, and nuts) in my time. I don't have many dreams or dramatic spiritual experiences, and if I do, it is usually due to too much pizza before I go to bed. Yet, on the morning of September 11, 2001, I had one I will never forget.

I had gone to bed at my usual time the night before and slept peacefully through the night as I almost always do. The next morning, though, I awoke from a deep sleep in tears. I don't mean that I was somewhat tearful as though from a dream that moved me. I mean that I was weeping as though grief had possessed my soul.

It confused me and left me disoriented for a while. I wandered about the house, and only after trying to clear my mind did I finally make it to the office for an important meeting. But I couldn't stop weeping, and I called my wife to ask her to pray. Not long after, one of my staff came to my office and told me to turn on the television. I couldn't believe what I saw before me. The first image that formed on my screen was what I now know to be the second plane to hit the World Trade Center. I knew, then, why my spirit was grieving even while I slept.

When that horrible day of infamy occurred, people began saying, "We live in a new world now. It will never be the same again." They were trying to get their minds around the fact that such horrors must signal a new era, that people would surely never feel safe again. As right as they might have been about people feeling safe again in our generation, they were wrong that this was anything new. The truth is, it was very old. A battle that has been raging for centuries merely crashed into our lives. A war waged in nations around the world merely exploded onto our Western landscape. It is the war between Islam and Christian civilization.

ISLAM AND THE DESTINY OF AMERICA

I cannot tell you how important it is that we understand the true nature of Islam, that we see it for what it really is. In fact, I will tell you this: I do not believe our country can truly fulfill its divine purpose until we understand our historical conflict with Islam. I know that this statement sounds extreme, but I do not shrink from its implications. The fact is that America was founded, in part, with the intention of seeing this false religion destroyed, and I believe

September 11, 2001, was a generational call to arms that we can no longer ignore. Consider the evidence.

It was to defeat Islam, among other dreams, that Christopher Columbus sailed to the New World in 1492. He was a young boy when the devastating news of the fall of Constantinople to Muslim armies reached his land. It marked him. He grew into manhood surrounded by tales of the Crusades into Muslim lands. When he determined to fulfill Marco Polo's dream and return to the east by sailing west, he did so in part to harvest the wealth of the New World to liberate the Old World from Islam. As he wrote to Isabella and Ferdinand from the Americas on his first voyage:

> I hope to God that when I come back here from Castile…that I will find…gold…in such quantities that within three years the Sovereign will prepare for and undertake the reconquest of the Holy Land. I have already petitioned Your Highnesses to see that all the profits of this, my enterprise, should be spent on the conquest of Jerusalem, and Your Highnesses smiled and said that the idea pleased them, and that even without the expedition they had the inclination to do it.[1]

Columbus dreamed of defeating the armies of Islam with the armies of Europe made mighty by the wealth of the New World. It was this dream that, in part, began America.

What Columbus dreamed became the hope of later generations. The greatest theologian of the American colonial era, and possibly of American history, was Jonathan Edwards. In his *History of Redemption,* written in 1773, Edwards predicted that a great revival to begin at the dawn of the twenty-first century in America would spell the end of Islam. What Edwards called "Mahometanism" would fall, he wrote, "when the Spirit begins to be so gloriously poured forth" at the end of the age.

Satan's Mahometan kingdom shall be utterly over-
thrown. And then—though Mahometanism has
been so vastly propagated in the world, and is upheld by such a great empire—this smoke, which has
ascended out of the bottomless pit, shall be utterly
scattered before the light of that glorious day, and
the Mahometan empire shall fall at the sound of the
great trumpet which shall then be blown.[2]

This expectation of the fall of Islam was a central theme of the
Great Awakening, the founding revival of the Revolution, and thus
became a central theme in what might be called the founding dream
of America.

It must have come as no surprise to those who fought it, then,
that America's first war was against Muslim armies. Modern Americans are often shocked to hear this. They assume that our first war
was against the British in the War of 1812. Not so. Our first war
was the Tripolitan War, fought against the Muslim pirates of North
Africa's Barbary Coast. It was a war that presaged much in our history, complete with hostages, rescue missions, terrorist acts, and a
Congress that could not decide whether it was engaged in a war or a
police action.

Though later generations would tend to see this and most wars
in nonspiritual terms, Americans of that generation understood their
battle as the Rais Hudga Mahomet Salamia did. He was the Muslim captain of a ship manned by American captives at the start of
the war. He warned his enslaved crew of Christians that they were
to be treated harshly, "for your history and superstition in believing
in a man who was crucified by the Jews, and disregarding the true
doctrine of God's last and greatest Prophet Mahomet."[3] Clearly, the
Tripolitan War was a battle of faiths, and Americans are reminded of
this deeply religious conflict every time the U.S. Marines tell us in
song that they were fashioned first "on the shores of Tripoli."

THE CHALLENGE OF ISLAM TODAY

Other examples of America's historic conflict with Islam could be cited, but the point is made. September 11 calls us to understand afresh a struggle that is deeply rooted in our past. It is a struggle with more than terrorism, more than embittered third world nations. It is a fundamental conflict between the founding values of the West and the inherent worldview of a religious system quite at odds with them. This, in our age of religious syncretism, is hard to understand, but we find now we have no choice. The time has come.

In fact, we may already be losing the battle. As I scan the world, I find that Islam is responsible for more pain, more bloodshed, and more devastation than nearly any other force on earth at this moment. I look to the horrors of Sudan, and I find slavery, massacre, and traumatic human upheaval of the sort that even beleaguered Africa has seldom seen. Nigeria, on a smaller scale, is much the same. The hand-to-hand violence in the streets of Indonesia has astonished the world. The informed know that the Taliban had been sending refugees by the thousands over the border of Pakistan for years before the recent crisis. And not long ago, the world was horrified to hear that more than 150 children were killed and nearly 250 more hospitalized when Muslim Chechen rebels commandeered a school in Russia.

If I spoke of the persecution of Christians by Muslims, I could broaden even further the scope of what I am saying. I will limit myself to Muslims against Muslims. The world is scarcely aware that some three hundred thousand Kurds were butchered under sanction of clerical *fatwa,* or religious decree, in Iraq. Before that, the war between Iran and Iraq was enflamed by the declared jihads of Shiite against Sunni, Sunni against Shiite. This was the world's bloodiest war, in a long and tortured history of bloody wars. The list could continue for pages.

There are some, of course, who will say that the violence I cite is the exception and not the rule. I beg to differ. I will counter, respectfully, that what some call "extremists" are instead mainstream believers who are drawing from the well at the very heart of Islam. It was said of Ishmael and his descendants in ancient times that they would "live by the sword," that he was "a wild donkey of a man; his hand will be against everyone and everyone's hand against him, and he will live in hostility toward all his brothers."[4] I suggest that this is the spirit that has come to fill Islam or perhaps that Islam encompassed from the beginning.

This would be nothing to worry about if Islam was just a backwater religion on the fringe of history. But it is not. Unless Islam is checked from without and reformed, at the least, from within, it will become a force that shapes the future of our world as much as any other on earth. Do you know that since September 11, 2001, some 34,000 Americans have become Muslims? This means that thousands of Americans have embraced the very religion that inspired the worst assault on their country in a generation. Did you know that there are some 1,209 mosques in America, 25 percent of which have been built since 1994? And did you know that there are nearly a billion and a half Muslims in the world? But how would we know this—after all, it's not in *People* magazine or on *Access Hollywood*. All these statistics do not bode well if Islam is what I believe it to be.[5]

There is another statistic that should give us a jolt, too. Did you know that Islam is the fastest-growing religion in the world? Some dispute this, I know, but it is true if you consider how Islam is growing. There is no question that Christianity is growing by conversion more rapidly than any other religion in the world. Nearly 250,000 people convert to Christianity every day worldwide. However, the Christian part of the world is shrinking overall, largely because of abortion. The fact is that Europe, for example, is aborting itself to death. The Muslims of Europe, who do not practice abortion, are increasing as a percentage of population at an astonishing rate, as they are worldwide. So this explains Islam's growth. It is literally growing itself by birthrates into the largest and fastest-growing religion on earth. In fact, by the year 2025, Muslims will comprise 30 percent of the world's population.[6]

To give you a better picture of Islam, take a look at where con-
centrations of Muslims exist around the world. Islam is growing in
some of the world's most strategic locations. Consider the following:
As I said before, in round numbers, there are some one and one-half
billion Muslims in the world. Only about six million of these live in
the United States. The five largest Muslim nations are Indonesia with
180 million, Pakistan with 125 million, Bangladesh with 109 million, India with 84 million, and Iran with 66 million. Some of the
countries we think of as Muslim strongholds are somewhat lower on
the list. Sudan and Afghanistan each have 22 million Muslims, Iraq
has 20 million, and Saudi Arabia has 19 million.[7]

The facts are clear, then. We are heading toward a historic conflict. Islam is growing rapidly and is becoming more violent. America
has historically understood herself as a bastion against Islam in the
world. Now, America is engaged in conflict with Muslims at home
and on the far-flung battlefields of Afghanistan and Iraq. Clearly, history is crashing in upon us.

Yet what makes this conflict with Islam so desperate is that Islam
is not just another belief system at odds with Christianity. It is not
just a set of superstitions or practices that people do in the privacy of
their own homes that never bother anyone else. Islam is, instead, a
faith that fully intends to conquer the world. It cannot be ignored. It
must be answered. But first, it must be understood.

ISLAM 101

If you will allow me, I want to teach you about Islam. Most people in
America have no idea what Islam teaches. In fact, just after the tragedies of September 11, 2001, some Americans proved just how ignorant of Islam they were. In one city, a Jewish synagogue had rocks
thrown through its windows because some youths could not distinguish a synagogue from a mosque. In another city, several Sikhs were
beaten up by people who assumed they were Muslim. These are just
a few examples. Americans can tell you who J.Lo married last week,
recite verbatim the lyrics of Britney's latest song, or tell you a dozen

"You might be a redneck, if…" jokes. Yet, the fact is that Americans are woefully ignorant of other faiths. This is not only tragic, but when it comes to Islam, now the greatest religious enemy of our civilization in the world, it is also dangerous.

So, let me teach you the basics of Islam. At the outset, I must state three important truths that I hope to provide support for in the following pages.

1. The God of Christianity and the god of Islam are two separate beings.

2. Muhammad received revelations from demons and not from the true God.

3. Islam is an anti-Christ religion that intends, through violence, to conquer the world.

These truths may sound extreme to you, but they are true. I trust that by the time you finish reading these pages, you will see that what I have said is true.

Islam began with a man named *Muhammad* who was born in A.D. 570 in the Arabian town of Mecca.[8] This city is important to our story. In those days, Mecca was a thriving market town and the center of worship for the Arab people. The religious heart of Mecca was an area that encircled a black building called the *Ka'aba.* This building was holy to the Arabs because it housed a meteorite called the *Black Stone.* In the ancient world, meteorites were considered to be holy objects sent from heaven. All the Arab tribes worshiped their individual gods around this Ka'aba, which meant that more than 270 gods were honored there. One of these gods, but only one among the many, was Allah. He was the god of the Quraysh tribe, who believed that this Allah was the only true god. Muhammad was a member of this tribe.

Muhammad had an unusual upbringing. His father died before he was born, and his mother died shortly after giving birth. Muhammad's uncle, Abu Talib, raised him and taught him the skills of a caravan leader. He was a lonely child, an epileptic who often cried himself to sleep at night on the cold desert floor.

His travels took him to the far reaches of the Middle East and gave him opportunity to learn about the many religions of the ancient world. He quickly realized that the Jews and the Christians had a comprehensive faith that made them great and powerful, while the Arabs had only their many tribal gods and were, in truth, not unified as a people at all.

Muhammad came into the employ of a wealthy widow named Khadija. Though she was fifteen years older than he, over time the two fell in love and married. Muhammad found himself a prosperous, respected merchant with an adoring wife and a growing family.

Yet he was still troubled by the religious problems of the Arabs. He often went to the mountains outside of Mecca to pray and ponder this matter of faith. Once, when he was meditating in a cave on a peak of Mt. Hira in A.D. 610, he had the experience that became the foundation of a new faith that would sweep the world.[9]

While prostrate on the floor of his cave one night, deep in meditation, he heard a voice. "Recite!" it said. Muhammad was confused and alarmed. It was a spirit, surely. He could feel its presence filling the cave, or maybe the whole mountain. He believed it was a demon and suspected it had mistaken him for one of the ecstatic prophets, sometimes called a "reciter," a *kahin*. But he was not and had no intention of becoming one.

"I am not a reciter," he insisted aloud, believing the spirit mistook him for another man.

And for a moment there was nothing. But then, in a violent rush, the unseen spirit gripped him and overwhelmed him with such pressure that he thought he was going to die. Suddenly, it let him go. There was a pause. Then, as firmly as before, the spirit demanded: "Recite!"

Again Muhammad replied, "I am not a reciter." Yet again, the spirit gripped him until the crush was more than he could bear. Release came, then another pause. Muhammad was angry and scared, certain the spirit was wrong about him. It was no compliment to be called a *kahin*, and Muhammad knew it. He was revolted to be thought among them and resisted.

Again the spirit spoke: "Recite!"

Again Muhammad replied: "I am no reciter."

And again the invisible but horrifying grip that must lead to death. Then...nothing.[10]

But the voice came again, and Muhammad found that the spirit was speaking through his own mouth: "Read! (or Proclaim!) in the name of your Lord and Cherisher, Who created—created man, out of a (mere) clot of congealed blood: He Who taught (the use of) the Pen, taught man that which he did not know."[11]

Now Muhammad felt certain this was a mistake, for after all, he could learn nothing by the pen—he was illiterate, as were many in his day. The spirit was wrong. But Muhammad had spoken the words despite himself, spoken what he did not understand and had not conceived in his mind. He was possessed, certainly. It had happened. He was a mad *kahin* despite himself.

In a rush of terror he ran from the cave. He found a summit and was just about to throw himself off when the voice came again: "O Muhammad! Thou art the apostle of God, and I am Gabriel."[12] He stopped, now more confused than ever but trying to understand. He was breathless and frantic. What should he do? In a flash, he decided. He would go to his wife. She would know. She could tell him if he were mad or, worse, possessed.

Crawling on hands and knees, his whole body convulsed, he arrived home and fell into Khadija's lap. He begged her to cover him with a blanket or a shawl. She did, but now he looked more like a *kahin* than ever, for the ecstatic prophets always covered themselves before delivering an oracle. Had he become one himself? He shared what had happened to him with Khadija and asked her if he were indeed possessed.

She assured him, "Rejoice, O dear husband, and be of good cheer. You will be the Prophet of this people."[13]

Muhammad knew what this meant. For he was of the Quraysh tribe, a people deeply devoted to Allah. The name means "the god," but this deity was merely one of the many worshiped at the Ka'aba. For the Quraysh, though, Allah was primary, and Muhammad knew that if he was a prophet at all, then he must be a prophet of Allah.

Still, could he be mistaken? Could he be possessed? Khadija protested, "You are kind and considerate toward your kin. You help the poor and forlorn and bear their burdens. You are striving to restore the high moral qualities that your people have lost. You honor the guest and go to the assistance of those in distress. This cannot be, my dear."[14]

He wanted to believe but was unsure. Khadija saw his doubt, and it sparked an idea. She would go to her cousin Waraqa, a Christian who was wise in such matters and would give advice. She ran quickly to find the blind old man and told him the story. When he heard what had befallen Muhammad, he cried, "Holy, holy! By Him in whose hand is the soul of Waraqa, there hath come unto Muhammad the greatest Namus (Name), even he that would come unto Moses. Verily Muhammad is the Prophet of this people. Bid him rest assured."[15]

Something in the Christian's words settled the matter. Upon hearing Khadija repeat what the old man had said, Muhammad resigned himself—he was indeed to be the prophet of his people, a prophet of Allah. He was reluctant but willing. Soon there were more trips to the mountain, more revelations. They came like the clanging of bells and often left him shaken and feverish. But the spirit spoke again and again. This spirit, this Gabriel, told Muhammad that Allah, the god of the Quraysh, was more than a local deity, more than just one of hundreds, but rather the lord of creation, the god of all men. And so they must know; they must be converted. This Allah must be given due honor and must be obeyed. Men must submit to their true lord.

These words became the meaning of Muhammad's life, his answer for his people, and his message to the world: "There is no god but Allah, and I, Muhammad, am his Prophet."

Now, this is the story of Islam's beginning. Muhammad had an experience with his tribal god, and it told him he was a prophet. Muhammad thought the spirit was a demon and almost killed himself out of fear that he was possessed. A Christian told him he was hearing from God, though, so Muhammad came to believe that he was hearing from the only true God and that he was this God's only true prophet.

Before I show you what Islam teaches, let me make a couple of matters clear from the story you have just read. First, Muhammad did not hear from the true God, the Father of our Lord Jesus Christ. Muhammad heard from a demon spirit, which portrayed itself as a tribal deity. This god was but one of the hundreds worshiped at the Ka'aba and was the god of Muhammad's tribe. What I want you to see is that any comparison to Jehovah—the Creator of the universe, the God of the Old and New Testaments, and the God of Jesus Christ—is fiction. Allah was a demon spirit. Even Muhammad thought so at first.

I want you to also notice the way in which the spirit manifested itself to Muhammad. It did not come in peace and truth, as the angels and messengers of the true God did in Scripture. Instead, it came in violence, fear, control, and domination. It forced its will upon Muhammad with such oppression that Muhammad thought he was losing his mind. This is not the way of a true messenger of the true God, as we see in the Old and New Testaments.

Finally, though, I want you to consider what effect this had on Muhammad. This man, sadly convinced by a Christian that he was hearing from God, continued to have revelations. They would come on him with a gripping fear. He would hear the sounds of loud bells in his head, and they would force the breath from him. When a revelation ended, Muhammad would be left in a fitful fever for days on end. These signs befit a man who is gripped by a demon, but not a man who has had a revelation from the true God. We see nothing of such occurrences in the Bible or in the annals of Church history. Muhammad was tragically beset by a demon, which he mistook for the living God. He thus became the mouthpiece of a conspiracy of spiritual evil.

THE FIVE ARTICLES OF FAITH

Now, before we draw some conclusions about Islam in our modern world, let me survey the beliefs most Muslims hold dear. It is fairly easy to understand the basic tenets of Islam because every Muslim is supposed to subscribe to "Five Articles of Faith." This makes our task easy. Let's see what these Articles of Faith are.

1. Belief in God

We have already seen that the god of Islam, Allah, was a tribal deity that Muhammad insisted was the only true God. In fact, Allah is a demon spirit, and Muhammad became a demonized man. This basic fact is the foundation for the evil that Islam is foisting on the world, as we will see.

2. Belief in angels

Since Gabriel, whom the Arabs call *Jibril*, gave many revelations to Muhammad, angels figure fairly prominently in the Muslim scheme. These angels, though, are not the beings we see pictured in Christian art. Gabriel, for example, is simply the spirit of truth. In fact, many Muslims believe he is the Holy Spirit. He, like all angels in Islam, is made of light and has no physical body.

Muslims believe that there are two angels assigned to each person. One records good deeds, and the other records bad deeds. This has given rise to the picture we sometimes see in comedies of an angel on one shoulder of a man and a devil on the other, each one urging him to evil or good. This is a parody of Islamic belief, though many think it comes from Christian teaching.

Among the angels there is an evil one called *al Shaitan*, clearly borrowed from the Christian belief in Satan. He is often pictured as a black dog. It is important to distinguish *al Shaitan* and all the angels in Islam from the *jinni*. These *jinni* are spirits that range somewhere between men and angels. They can do good or evil, but they are not angels or even fallen angels. We get our English word *genie* from these *jinni*, and we probably know them best from stories of Aladdin or *Tales From the Arabian Nights*. It should not be surprising to us that a religion begun in a demonic manifestation should have such a preoccupation with spirits.

3. Belief in Scripture

The Quran is the holy book, the "standing miracle," of Islam. It is supposedly the compiled revelations of Muhammad, but here is an important myth we must expose.

Remember that Muhammad was illiterate. He wrote nothing during his life. Though he had dozens, if not hundreds, of revelations and presumably preached thousands of sermons, he left nothing of the written word. When he died, the teachings of Islam existed only in the secondhand notes of his followers, in the words they had committed to memory, and in the common sayings that circulated orally in the Muslim community.

This meant that the business of gathering everything possible of the Prophet's words had to begin. The *ummah*, the Islamic community, began to piece together what they remembered of the Prophet's teaching and revelations. The work took decades and finally produced *al-qur'an*, (in the West, "the Quran") the "recitation." Scholars agree that it did not exist until A.D. 691 at the earliest—fifty-nine years after the Prophet's death. It would have 114 chapters, or *surahs*, organized from the longest to the shortest. In these surahs, Allah would speak in the first person, and he would speak only in Arabic. This was a reward to the Arabs for turning to Allah. He had said to them: "Do you ask for a greater miracle than this, O unbelieving people, than to have your language chosen as the language of that incomparable Book, one piece of which puts all your golden poetry to shame?"

I want you to think about what the Quran really is. Muhammad didn't write it. His followers wrote it after he was dead, and then only from their memory and scrawled notes. This explains why the Quran is full of so many contradictions. The truth is that the Quran is one confusing document. You can't even discern what happened at Muhammad's death—there are conflicting accounts even of that important event. You also find conflicting views of some very important doctrines. For example, the Quran says to kill Jews and Christians, but it *also* says to let them live in peace because they are a "people of the book," meaning the Bible. No wonder we hear Muslims saying completely opposite things about their faith!

It is vital that you do not miss this point: the Quran is only authoritative in Arabic. In any other language, the Quran is unofficial and unsuitable for doctrine. Consider the implications of this. Only 30 percent of all Muslims worldwide are literate, and, of these, fewer still can read classical Arabic. This means that the vast majority of Muslims, well above 70 percent, cannot read the book that created their religion. It also means that for them, Islam is what the Muslim leaders say it is. This is where a great deal of the radicalism in Islam finds its origin.

The Quran isn't the only holy book of Islam, though. There is the *hadith*, an additional collection of the sayings of Muhammad. Muslims also revere the *Torah* of Moses, the psalms (*Zabin*) of David, and the Gospels of Jesus (*Injil*). Each of these, of course, must be interpreted in light of the Quran.

This makes for some interesting conclusions. For example, Muslims believe that Ishmael was Abraham's child of promise, not Isaac. It is the descendants of Ishmael, the Arabs, who are the chosen race, and the Torah would have said this had not the Jews distorted its message. It is no wonder that Islam supports such vehement hatred of the Jews. Muslims believe the Jews have stolen their "promise." There is even a selective approach to what the Gospels say about Jesus. Islam maintains that Jesus was born of a virgin, did miracles, and was a prophet. Yet, He is not the Son of God and certainly is not divine.

Again, had the Christians left the Gospels uncorrupted, the truth would never have been hidden, Muslims believe.

4. Belief in the prophets

In Islam, Muhammad is the Seal of the Prophets, the last and greatest in a series. Before him came Adam, Noah, Abraham, Moses, and Jesus. This may seem an odd list at first, but it is this inclusion of prophets past that has helped Islam spread so rapidly.

Let me explain. Part of the fuel that powers Islam's advance is its syncretism, the way it incorporates elements of other faiths. Islam tells a Jew he can keep Abraham, Moses, the Torah, and the psalms when he becomes a Muslim. It tells a Christian he can hold to Jesus, the Gospels, and large portions of his Old Testament heritage, yet be a Muslim. This is inviting to those who may be uncertain about their faith in the first place or who are faced with death if they don't convert.

5. The doctrine of the Last Day

This was a strange doctrine to the Arabs who, before Muhammad, had no belief in an afterlife. Muhammad taught that the faithful enter paradise, a place of pleasure. I want you to see what an evil thing this doctrine of paradise is.

In this place of reward, the obedient will recline on soft couches, drinking wine from jeweled goblets. They will be tended by *houras*, or maidens of paradise, with whom the men may mate as freely as they please. The Quran also mentions that boys of alabaster skin will tend the faithful in paradise, and some have taken this to mean that pederasty will be one of the blessings of Allah, though the meaning is unclear. The state of women in paradise is also uncertain. They may be refashioned into the *houras* to tend the men, or they may have some other rewards that are not specified. Their place in the afterlife is never clearly defined.

In other words, Muslims will be rewarded in paradise with pleasures that are forbidden them on earth. What perversion this is! Only the objectification of women in an MTV rap video, or a visit to Hugh Hefner's house of hedonism, known as the "Playboy Mansion," or the images spawned by the burgeoning pornography industry seem to be its equal.

It is important to note that there is no certainty about the afterlife for any Muslim. He does not have what the Christian would call "assurance." He lives his life doing as many good deeds as possible, and when the books recorded by the angels are opened on the day of judgment, he will be told whether he may enter paradise. If he has not qualified, he will suffer in the fires of hell, but only temporarily, it seems. In time, he will be released.

The important issue to understand is that Islam offers no certainty. This plays a major role in two matters we will discuss later—jihad and terrorism.

6. Belief in fate, or kismet

Though there are only the Five Articles of Faith, there is, somewhat unofficially, a sixth. It is the belief in fate, or *kismet*. The Muslim believes so much in Allah's control over creation that he views everything that happens as a result of Allah's decrees. What happens tomorrow is not a direct result of actions today. What happens is a result of what Allah decrees.

Some historians have suggested that this idea of kismet has, until recently, kept the Islamic world from developing economically. Progress is hardly possible where a people do not believe that good will necessarily come from hard work, for example, or that planting today will likely mean harvesting tomorrow. Others maintain that kismet is simply a hedge against pride, against the assumption that man determines his own destiny. It is a caution that applies even to small matters. If an American calls his Muslim friend in Istanbul and asks, "Will you pick me up for lunch tomorrow?" he will not hear a firm yes.

The orthodox Muslim will say, "Inshallah, I will pick you up," which means "If Allah wills." This same word, *Inshallah*, is what one hears when he asks a Muslim farmer if it will rain or when he asks if the tribes will stop fighting. "Inshallah," is the answer, which is another way of saying "Perhaps, but I don't want to dishonor Allah by saying so."

This, then, is what a Muslim must believe. He must believe in Allah and the angels who do his bidding. He must accept his words, receive his prophets, honor Muhammad above all men, and hope for the glories of paradise.

THE FIVE PILLARS OF THE FAITH

Yet paradise is not won by believing alone. It is earned in large part by the doing. What a Muslim believes frames his understanding of what he must do. Remember that Islam is a restoration of *righteous doing* as much and perhaps a bit more than it is a restoration of *right believing*. Here, then, in a list that has come to be called the *Pillars of the Faith*, is what a Muslim must do.

1. He must first recite the Creed of Islam, the **Shahada.**

It is, as is all of Islam, quite simple: "There is no God but Allah, and Muhammad is his prophet." This is what a man says to become a Muslim, and it is what he repeats in prayers and affirmations thousands of times throughout his life. It is whispered into his ears when he is born and as he dies. It is the only formal creed in Islam, astonishingly concise when compared with the volumes of creeds produced down through the centuries by Christians.

If there is an intelligence behind the religion of Islam, we see its genius here. It was said of the British Navy that it was a system designed by geniuses to be run by idiots. The idea was that brilliance simplified and systematized for the least able assured that the brilliance would survive. This is Islam. Conceived in a land of illiterates, in a world of oral transmission and simple tales of broad meaning, Islam codified itself in a pregnant vocabulary that was forever giving birth. There are religions of the world at risk of perishing for want of incarnation into such a simple formula as, "There is no God but Allah, and Muhammad is his prophet."

2. A Muslim must also devote himself to prayer, or salat.

At first, Muhammad asked men to pray twice a day, then it was three times, and finally it became the five times a day now practiced the world over. The Prophet also required men to turn toward Jerusalem at first, in imitation of Jewish rituals, but in time he set Mecca as the place of holy affection.

It is an impressive sight wherever it takes place. A man spreads a newspaper on the grass in a San Diego oceanfront park and bows on it to the god of the Ka'aba. Three hundred South African Muslims kneel side by side in the Johannesburg airport at four in the afternoon, their flight to Dubai delayed while they finish *salat*. A lone Muslim climbs to the rooftop of his Amman shop, spreads his prayer carpet, and devotes himself once again to the god of Muhammad. *Salat* may well be the grand unifying ritual of Islam.

We should be careful to understand that this form of prayer is not a matter of prayer lists or making needs known. *Salat* is devotion, asking Allah to make the worshiper even more submitted and pure than he is. The Muslim prays an intercessory formula, a progression of devotion and cleansing, that is the same each time, fives times a day, all his life. This is not a creative expression. This is the offering of submission to the one who must be obeyed.

An example of what a Muslim prays is found in the first surah of the Quran. This is called *Al-Fatiha* and comprises the most prayed words in Islam: "In the name of Allah, Most Gracious, Most Merciful. Praise be to Allah, the Cherisher and Sustainer of the Worlds; Most Gracious, Most Merciful; Master of the Day of Judgment. You do we worship, and Your aid we seek. Show us the straight way" (Surah 1:1–6). This, in essence, is the Lord's Prayer of Islam.

3. A Muslim must also give alms, or zakat.

Though there is no fixed requirement, approximately one-fortieth, or about 2.5 percent, of all a man owns is meant to be given to the poor and the needy. Interestingly, only a small percentage of Christians worldwide give evidence of obeying the biblical injunction to give

10 percent of their income to God's work. Perhaps this percentage would increase if Christian countries did what some Muslims countries do. In many Muslim regions, the *zakat* is legally demanded.

This requirement produces an interesting brand of beggar in some Muslim countries. The beggar knows that the one who gives is earning paradise by his generosity. He is doing himself a favor by giving. The beggar, then, very often feels no sense of gratitude or obligation to the giver. On the contrary, he believes that the giver should feel himself fortunate that he has someone to give to. Westerners who give to the poor in Muslim countries are often shocked to be met with a kind of grudging silence that comes from the poor man believing that his Western benefactor is only serving himself.

4. A Muslim must also fast, or sawm.

During the same month of the year in which Muhammad was visited by Jibril, the Muslim eats or drinks nothing during daylight hours. This lasts for the thirty days of the month of Ramadan. Muslims are also required to read through the Quran by completing one-thirtieth of the holy book every day. The highlight is the Night of Power, the night believed to be the anniversary of Muhammad's visitation. On this night, Muslims throughout the world pray for illumination and revelation like Muhammad's.

As laudable as the observance of Ramadan may be, the almost humorous sidelight is the immense amount of food consumed during this month of fasting. Many Muslims reverse their schedules and sleep during the day in order to eat at night. And what eating it is! Huge feasts are held, and an entire catering industry earns its keep during this one month, much as some businesses in the West earn all their income during the month that stretches from Thanksgiving to Christmas.

5. Finally, a Muslim must make pilgrimage, or hajj.

Once during his lifetime, a Muslim is expected to make his way to Mecca, much as Arabs had done for centuries before Muhammad. The elderly or infirm can send someone in their stead, but it is essential to salvation that every Muslim appear in some form in the Holy City.

This *hajj* is perhaps the clearest relic of the ancient paganism that gave rise to Islam. There are rituals the faithful are expected to undergo that carry hardly any meaning for the modern Muslim, but that have simply survived the centuries. When a man on *hajj* approaches Mecca, he casts off his ordinary clothes and puts on two seamless garments. He walks barefoot and neither shaves nor cuts his nails. He visits the Ka'aba and the mosque that attends it, *al-Masjid al-Haram*. Like his fathers fourteen hundred years before, he walks around the Ka'aba seven times and kisses the Black Stone. Then there are the unusual traditions. The faithful run between Mt. Safa and Mt. Marwa seven times, visit Mt. Ararat, spend the night at Muzdalifa, and throw stones at the three pillars of Mina. The original meaning of some of these rituals is lost but remains embedded in the heritage of Islam.

JIHAD

Though these are the Five Pillars of Islam, there is another obligation the Muslim cannot ignore. This is *jihad*, the most controversial of Muhammad's teachings. *Jihad* literally means "struggle," but it is often interpreted as "holy war." Islam teaches that a man should struggle for righteousness in four *jihads*: the *jihad* of the tongue, the *jihad* of the hand, the *jihad* of the heart, and the *jihad* of the sword. The first three obviously pertain to the Muslim's battle for mastery over his actions and thoughts. These struggles are personal and speak to the issues of discipline and character.

The *jihad* of the sword is different, though. It is the calling on every believer to impress the will of Allah upon the world. As one scholar has written, "The faith, being so simple and straightforward, was not likely to be misunderstood. It did not require the creeds, councils, and canons of Christianity. It did not depend upon the philosophical speculations of Judaism. It did not demand the cryptic mathematical calculations of Zoroastrianism. To Muhammad's mind, the only possible reason men or nations might resist or reject Allah's plain revelation was obstinate rebellion. Such recalcitrance had to be dealt with harshly, lest it spread its complex perversions far and wide. Infidelity had to be destroyed."[16]

Jihad is the war the righteous fight to claim the world for Allah. This is no battle for hearts and minds. It is a battle for absolute submission. And it is a battle won by the shedding of blood. On this the Quran is clear. Consider these quotations from the Quran that teach religious violence and global terror.

- "Muhammad is the Messenger of Allah; and those who are with him are strong against Unbelievers [another translation reads, 'the infidels'], (but) compassionate amongst each other" (Surah 48:29).

- "Fight [another translation reads, 'Declare war upon'] those who do not believe in Allah nor the Last Day, nor hold that forbidden which has been forbidden by Allah and His Messenger, nor acknowledge the Religion of Truth, (even if they are) of the People of the Book, until they pay the Jizya with willing submission, and feel themselves subdued. The Jews call 'Uzair a son of Allah, and the Christians call Christ the Son of Allah. That is a saying from their mouth; (in this) they but imitate what the Unbelievers of old used to say. Allah's curse be on them: how they are deluded away from the Truth!" (Surah 9:29–30).

- "As to those who reject faith, I will punish them with terrible agony in this world and in the Hereafter, nor will they have anyone to help" (Surah 3:56).

- "From those, too, who call themselves Christians, We did take a Covenant, but they forgot a good part of the Message that was sent them: so We estranged them, with enmity and hatred between the one and the other, to the Day of Judgment. And soon will Allah show them what it is they have done" (Surah 5:14).

- "And fight them on until there is no more tumult or oppression, and there prevail justice and faith in Allah altogether and everywhere..." (Surah 8:39).

There are dozens more passages like these throughout the Quran and the hadith. To read them is to understand that Islam calls the Muslim to peace...but only with his fellow Muslims. To the outsiders, to the Christians and the Jews and all who are the infidels, the message is simple: convert or die. It has been so since the beginning. Muhammad was once asked what deed was dearest to Islam. He responded, "Prayers, obedience to parents, and religious fighting, in that order."

This doctrine of *jihad* is one example of how Muhammad's teachings often evolved, changing to fit the circumstances of his day. When Islam was a fledgling movement, Muhammad urged peaceful persuasion. This theme is exemplified in Surah 16:125–126. Then, after the flight to Medina, Muhammad began to approve fighting to ward off aggression and to reclaim property confiscated by infidels. Surah 22:39 is evidence of this transition. Soon, caravan raiding became the primary material support for Muhammad's mission, and some scholars suggest that the *profit* motive now began to be more at work than the *Prophet* motive.

From that time on, Muhammad's teaching on *jihad* changed rapidly. First, he taught the righteousness of all defensive wars against Islam's enemies. Then, he taught that all who die in righteous conflict will go to paradise. Not long after, there was a shift from the righteousness of defensive war to the righteousness of offensive war against nonbelievers. The only restraint was a ban on fighting during the four months set aside for pilgrimage. In time, even this was lifted. *Jihad* in its final state became this: when commanded by a recognized Muslim leader, Muslims can attack nonbelievers in any season and on any land not yet surrendered to Islam. Thus, the famous Surah 9:29, which instructs the faithful to fight against Christians and Jews until they "feel themselves subdued."

It is absolutely essential to understand the appeal that *jihad* has for the faithful. Remember that Islam is a religion of externals. Amass enough right deeds, and Allah may allow you into paradise. But you are never sure. As I said before, there is none of what a Christian would call "assurance." In other words, a Muslim never knows if he has done enough to be accepted by Allah on the Day of Judgment. Thus, when Muhammad began to teach that all who die in righteous fighting go to paradise, he established the only means by which a Muslim can be certain of his place in eternity. This explains much that we experience in our world today. A teenager straps on a vest filled with explosives, walks into a Jerusalem restaurant, and blows himself up along with everyone within thirty yards. His parents rejoice. Not only has he struck a blow for the Palestinian cause, but also he is certainly in paradise. He is a martyr, received with honor in the courts of Allah. We can see then how much this doctrine of *jihad* is shaping the world in which we live.

This, then, is Islam. It is a polyglot, hybrid religion fashioned from the faiths Muhammad would have known from his travels and from the influences of the demonic in Muhammad's life. Yet, today, this odd religion is the fastest-growing one in the world.

THE DECEPTION OF ISLAM

Islam grows, though, on the power of deception. Let me take as an example of this deception the words of Queen Noor of Jordan as to why she became a Muslim. Queen Noor, you may remember, was the American wife of King Hussein of Jordan. She is a pretty, well-spoken woman who was educated at Princeton and who converted to Islam in order to marry the king.

In her best-selling book, *Leap of Faith*, she described why she became a Muslim. Listen carefully to the reasons she gave for her conversion:

> I admired Islam's emphasis on a believer's direct relationship with God, the fundamental equality of rights of all men and women.... Islam calls for fairness, tolerance, and charity.... I was attracted by its simplicity and call for justice. Islam is a very personal belief system.... Honesty, faithfulness and moderation are a few of the virtues that Islam calls for.[17]

The tragedy of these words is not just that this beautiful American woman believes them and thus embraces a false faith, but that many in this country and the world believe similar deceptions. Let's consider carefully what Queen Noor says.

First, she says that Islam emphasizes the believer's direct relationship with God. Little could be further from the truth. The Muslim perception of Allah is far from the Christian perception of God. Allah is clearly not personable but is so far above man that he is unknowable. He not only can't be known, but also he is unmoved by anything his creatures do. In fact, it is a heresy to associate Allah with any other being or to believe that any being can approach him. To do so is called *shirk,* which is a serious offense to Allah. Men are commanded to submit to him, to serve him, and to praise him, but they will never know him or, for that matter, be sure they can please him. Muslims proudly say that Allah is lord, *al Rabb,* and that they are his slaves, *Abd.* This is a far cry from the Jewish God who could be King David's friend or the Christian God who so loves that He sacrificed His own Son.

Remember this statement: there are ninety-nine names for Allah in Islam. Not one of them is love. Queen Noor is wrong. Islam offers no personal relationship with Allah. Islam offers submission to a religious code. In fact, the very name *Islam* means just this: "submission."

Queen Noor also says that Islam honors women. This is an astonishing lie. From the very beginning, Islam traumatized women. We can perhaps overlook the fact that Muhammad himself had dozens of wives and dozens more concubines. This may be offensive to modern Western sensibilities, but it was not that unusual for Muhammad's time. What was unusual then and is repulsive now is that he took wives from his associates, married his cousin, and often boasted that Allah gave him the strength to satisfy all of his wives in one night. He seemed preoccupied with sex, and he seemed to view women as property for pleasure. He married one girl, Aisha, when she was six years old. Then he waited to consummate the marriage—until the girl was nine!

One has only to look at the state of women in the Islamic world today to know that Islam enslaves rather than liberates women. Scan the news for the evidence. In Pakistan, a woman who wasn't properly covered had acid thrown in her face not long ago. In Saudi Arabia, a woman caught in adultery is killed. Her male lover is not. In Afghanistan, a husband goes to a doctor to describe his wife's symptoms, but he will not allow his wife to be examined, even when her health is at stake and the doctor is a female. Vaginal disfigurations, a primitive guarantee of sexual purity, are not uncommon in the Muslim world, and in more than one Muslim country it has been against the law to teach a female to read.

As to Queen Noor's assertion that Islam offers tolerance and justice, I hardly need to comment. Again, scan the world scene for a moment as you read these words. Whether we speak of the Sudan, Indonesia, world terrorism, the Philippines, or anti-Christian violence in Central Asia, Islam is hardly a force for world peace. Indeed, as I examine the world at this moment, I can find no other religion as responsible for violence as Islam. In fact, to say it another way, I find no Islamic culture anywhere in the world in which tolerance of any kind is practiced.

There are many things I could say about Islam as a religious system. I am a Christian leader, after all, and I am always ready to talk about the truth of Christianity, about salvation in Jesus, and about how every other faith offers a false hope. My purpose in this chapter, though, is to talk about Islam as a force in our world and how our nation must awaken to its meaning. I'll leave confronting Islam with Christian apologetics to another day.

It is more important that I talk about our nation's confrontation with Islam. One of the forces that has shaped us in the West, and particularly in America, is how we view religion. America was founded by men who hoped to be free of the religious wars of Europe. They wanted a better way of dealing with faith than the bloodletting they had known. They decided that tolerance was best—that a man should be valued for what he could do regardless of what he believed. It worked, for the most part, and has allowed America to avoid religious bloodshed to a remarkable degree.

There is a danger with this approach, though, and it is the possibility that religion will not be taken as seriously as it ought. We have in essence said that in order to be friends with a man, we may have to diminish the importance of what he believes. This can lead to a diminishing of all religion and thus to a worldview that fails to consider the sway that faith holds on the hearts of men.

We see this fairly clearly illustrated in American foreign policy. Because Americans believe that good men can live in harmony regardless of their faith, our approach to the world very often ignores the issue of religion. Officially, we think like nonreligious people and assume all other nations do as well.

But they don't, and often our policies fail as a result. For example, decades ago American forces removed a traditional leader in Vietnam and tried to replace him with a democratically elected man. But democracy does not spring naturally from Buddhist soil, and the

Vietnamese people felt no allegiance to someone who had power just because a majority of voters gave it to him. Disaster followed.

Other nations have understood the power of religion very well. The Japanese attacked Pearl Harbor on a Sunday morning because they knew that it was a holy day, whatever that might have meant at that time. The British smeared their railroad tracks with pig fat during World War I in order to keep Arab Muslims, whose religion forbids the touching of pork, from destroying their railways. And how many wars against Israel have begun on the Jewish Sabbath?

Americans have a natural distaste for using a man's religion against him. It smacks of bigotry. But the fact is that you cannot address a people's behavior unless you address their religion, and never has this been so much the case as it is now. Islam is, as we have seen, a religion that teaches the violent subjugation of all non-Muslims. It promises paradise to terrorists and makes the vilest deed a thing of beauty in the eyes of Allah. For peace to prevail, these ideas have to be confronted, and this means that what our president calls *the war against terror* will have to include battle against the *beliefs* as well as the *actions* of violent Muslims if there is to be any success.

This is all the more the case given that most Muslims cannot read the Quran and know only what their mullah teaches them. It means that the ignorance factor is high and that an aggressive program of religious education could produce good fruit. Of course, we will risk the ire of our oil-producing Muslim friends, and that may require that we rethink our energy policies. Still, we are already living in an untenable inconsistency. We cannot continue to befriend without reservation the primary financiers of the very faith that is threatening to destroy us or at least make the world a harrowing place for generations to come.

Whether to fulfill the dreams of the Christian faith, the principles of a democratic society, or simply the priority of peace, Islam has to be confronted, and it has to be confronted at a religious and intellectual level. This means that the West will have to reexamine its own religious moorings and perhaps reclaim them. Are we a Christian nation? I say *yes*, but not a very good one. In order to reflect true Christian values, we need to become familiar with the Christian consensus that guided those who founded our nation.

Then we need to understand Islam, not just as a cultural force but as a flawed religion, filled with inconsistencies, that sanctions most of the violence in the world. The men and women who frame our foreign policy do not need to think that the First Amendment keeps them from understanding and contending with our enemies at a religious level. We cannot win the war against terror or the religious enemies of our nation any other way.

Finally, the schools and churches of our nation need to teach world religions instead of focusing on agenda items such as reproductive rights and distributing condoms instead of convictions. For public schools, this change would simply be part of producing well-educated citizens of the world. For Christian schools and churches, this is simply a matter of making sure our students know the times and know what the people of God should do. It is also a matter of inoculating the next generation against the enemies of the Christian faith.

We can win the war against terrorism, and we can see the transformation of Islam in our time. We cannot do it, however, with military might alone. We can do it only as we fight ideas with ideas, faith with faith, and cultural fruit with cultural fruit. We must, as you will hear me often say in this book, be "silent no more."

ACTION POINTS

- Be informed about how Islam started and what it stands for.

- Prayerfully read the Quran for yourself to understand the deception it contains.

- Log on to some of the better Web sites that track Islam in the world. These include www .e-prism.org and www.prophetofdoom.net.

- Recommended reading:
  The Cross and the Crescent: Christianity and Islam From Muhammad to the Reformation, by Richard Fletcher[18]

  What You Need to Know About Islam and Muslims, by George W. Braswell Jr.[19]

  The Blood of the Moon, by George Grant[20]

- Urge your pastor to make sure that world religions are taught in Sunday school.

- Make sure your home has a handbook on cults and world religions—McDowell and Stewart's *Handbook of Today's Religions* is a good one to start with.[21]

CHAPTER 6

EDUCATION:
Recovering Our Lost Legacy
SILENT NO MORE

> Knowledge is proud that he has learned so much;
> wisdom is humble that he knows no more.
>
> —WILLIAM COWPER

Knowledge is not all that it is cracked up to be. In fact, it is obvious that knowledge can be grossly overrated. As Mark Twain once quipped, "I've known many a soul educated to the point of total uselessness."[1] And as Samuel Johnson asserted, "A little knowledge is a dangerous thing. It only hastens fools to rush in where angels fear to tread."[2] Or, as the apostle Paul wrote, "Knowledge puffeth up."[3]

After all, knowledge can be transferred. Facts can be memorized. Curricula can be mastered. Information can be gathered. Disciplines can be learned. Data can be catalogued. Skills can be gained. But traditional education techniques can only go so far—truth and wisdom are not so easily obtained.

For decades our educational system has emphasized gaining knowledge. We want our children to have knowledge of the world. We want them to have knowledge of the basic academic categories. And perhaps most importantly, we want them to have knowledge of the skills necessary for the job market. Ours is the information age, after all. So, communicating information—or knowledge—has been our primary aim and objective. We have assumed that if our children had a good grasp of the knowledge they need, they would be able to make their way in the world.

As renowned educator Leo Brennan has rightly observed, "We Americans are enthusiasts for education."[4] Though there may be an underlying "anti-intellectualism" in a few isolated circles, by and large we Americans place a heavy emphasis on the education of our children. We demand good teachers. We demand good textbooks. We demand good facilities. We demand good supplemental resources. We demand the best and the latest and the snazziest of everything academia has to offer.

Thus, we have spared no expense or effort in order to pour knowledge into the minds and lives of the next generation. Ours is one of the most extensive and expensive school systems the world has ever seen.[5] Spending—in inflation-adjusted dollars—has increased some 400 percent per pupil in the past thirty years.[6] Teacher salaries have more than doubled.[7] And the per capita number of support personnel has nearly quadrupled.[8] Education has, in fact, become the second-largest industry in the nation, with more than a quarter-trillion dollars spent every year, supporting nearly three million teachers and administrators.[9] School reform issues top the list of concerns of both taxpayers and public officials during nearly every election cycle.

So what do we have to show for all this? Alas, not nearly enough.

KNOWLEDGE IS NOT ENOUGH

With all of our emphasis on knowledge, it is the height of irony that we seem to know so little. We are swimming in an ocean of 24/7/365 information. But precisely because there is so much undifferentiated and undistinguished data in that vast ocean, we are often overcome by its waves and swells. And now, all too many of us are actually drowning in it. Indeed, the U.S. Department of Education has described our country's educational crisis with the startling phrase, "A nation at risk."[10] And for good reason.

Public education in this country is a dismal failure.[11] Johnny can't read, and Susie can't spell.[12] Willie can't write, and Alice can't add.[13] Teacher competency is down.[14] Administrative effectiveness is down.[15] Student advancement is down.[16] Test scores are down.[17] Everything to do with our public school system is down—everything, that is, except crime, drug abuse, illicit sex, and the cost to taxpayers.[18]

According to one study, as many as 90 million adults in this country are functionally illiterate.[19] An additional 35 million are aliterate— they can read a few basics with difficulty, but that is about all.[20] SAT score comparisons reveal an unbroken decline from 1963 all the way up until the time when the standards were actually lowered a few years ago.[21] Average verbal scores have fallen over fifty points, and mathematics scores have dropped nearly forty points.[22] A decade ago, one study of the 158 member nations of the United Nations showed that the United States ranked forty-ninth in basic literacy levels.[23]

That study revealed that nearly 40 percent of all American high school seniors could not draw inferences from written material; only one-fifth could write a persuasive essay; and less than one-third could solve an arithmetic problem requiring multiple steps.[24] Thirty-eight percent were unable to locate the Mississippi River on a map of the North American continent; 35 percent were not able to find the Rocky Mountains; and 42 percent could not identify their own home state.[25]

Now, I'm giving you a lot of numbers, but if you are missing my point, let me make it clear: things are really bad in American education.

Let me show you just how bad. A study found that 25 million high school graduates could not correctly identify the United States on an outline map of the world; 44 million were unable to find the Pacific Ocean; and some 61 million were not able to come within 500 miles of locating the nation's capital.[26]

One study revealed that nearly one-third of all graduating high school seniors were not able to identify the Declaration of Independence as marking the formal break between the American colonies and Great Britain; 28 percent did not know that Columbus discovered America in 1492—believing that the event occurred sometime between 1750 and 1850; and 32 percent were unable to name more than three past presidents.[27] If you think I'm making this up, just watch one of Jay Leno's Man in the Street interviews on *The Tonight Show*.

The shocking conclusion of another study was that nearly half of all Americans are so poorly educated that they cannot perform such relatively simple tasks as calculating the price difference between two items at the grocery store or filling out a job application at a fast-food restaurant. One observer illustrated this deficiency with this anecdote. She walked into a local fast-food establishment and asked the youth behind the counter for a half-dozen chicken nuggets. "Uh," the droopy-eyed adolescent responded, "we don't have that. We only have six, nine, and twelve."

I long to live in an America where my fast food doesn't have to begin with a numeric code ("I'd like a number three, please.") to keep from confusing or overtaxing the intellectual capability of the mystery person behind the drive-through order box. What if I don't want any drink with my heart attack in a paper sack? And how about replacing the automatic change maker with a teenager who can actually make change? I would settle for not-so-fast food if I knew that the food chain employee might someday acquire the skills necessary to climb the employment food chain.

A National Endowment for the Humanities study rued all of these facts together as a grave harbinger of national decline and disintegration: "Knowledge of the ideas that have molded us and the ideals that have mattered to us function as a kind of civic glue. By failing to transmit these ideas and ideals from one generation to the next, we risk dissolution of the bonds that unite us as a nation and as a free people."[28]

The sad reality is that most Americans are so poorly educated that they don't even know they are poorly educated. According to former Education Secretary Richard Riley, "Such data paints a picture of a society in which the vast majority of Americans do not know that they do not have the skills to earn a living in our increasingly technological society and international marketplace."[29]

We have spent the money, established the commissions, surveyed the problems, initiated the reforms, rewritten the curricula, hired the experts, and overhauled the entire educational system. And yet, nearly 45 percent of all the products of that system cannot even read the front page of the morning newspaper.[30]

How could this have possibly happened? If we live in the information age, why is so little information getting through? If we are so intent on imparting knowledge, why do we know so little?

Part of the reason may well be that we simply forgot that education is more than simply the transfer of knowledge. However important knowledge may be, true education involves something more. As the great Victorian pastor and social reformer Charles Haddon Spurgeon once wrote, "I would have everybody able to read and write and cipher; indeed, I don't think a man can know too much; but mark you, the knowing of these things is not education; and there are millions of your reading and writing folk who are as ignorant as neighbor Norton's calf."[31]

KNOWLEDGE IN CONTEXT

Those ignorant masses of whom Spurgeon speaks are not those who failed to finish their lessons. They are instead those who *did* finish—or rather those who naively thought that lessons were the sorts of things that *could* be finished. Education does not have an ending point, a polar extreme, a finish line, an outcome. Instead it is a deposit, an endowment, a promise, and even a small taste of the future.

All talk of education is for us a reminder that we have only just begun to learn how to learn. It is an affirmation that though our magnificent heritage has introduced us to the splendid wonders of literature, art, music, history, science, and ideas in the past—we have only *just* been introduced. A lifetime adventure in these vast arenas still awaits us. Indeed, the most valuable lessons that education can convey are invariably the lessons that never end. That is actually at the heart of the Christian philosophy of education—a philosophy that provoked the most remarkable flowering of art, music, litera- ture, science, and progress the world has ever seen. It is a philosophy rooted in a desire for wisdom and understanding, not just knowledge; a philosophy focused on putting knowledge in context; a philosophy in pursuit of truth.

The problem with our current approach to education is that we have apparently all but given up on truth, and we have begun to avoid wisdom like the plague. This is evident, Leo Brennan has argued, in the fact that "we engage in the eminently dubious process of what is barbarously known as standardization."[32]

The only solution, he said, is to "restore the basic educational ideals and principles" that provoked Western civilization's great flow- ering of culture in the first place: a strident emphasis on wisdom and not just on knowledge; on truth and not just information.[33] After all, as William Butler Yeats once quipped, "Education is not the filling of a pail but the lighting of a fire."[34] We have spent so much time, effort, energy, and money in trying to fill pails that fires have not been lit. We have emphasized knowledge at the expense of wisdom and truth.

KNOWLEDGE, UNDERSTANDING, AND WISDOM

The proverbial triad of educational attainment includes knowledge, understanding, and wisdom—which together ultimately lead to truth.[35] Each of these component parts of true education is actually distinctively different. Each bears its own peculiar fruit in the life of the student. And each is developed by a unique course of instruction.

Knowledge is simply the accumulation of facts. It is learning the ABCs of any given subject. It is gathering the building blocks of any particular discipline. This is the beginning place of all education. But it is just the beginning. Someone who has a firm grasp of the facts of math or science or literature but does not have any idea how those facts fit in with the rest of life is hardly any better off than the person who remains totally ignorant. Understanding is necessary in order to actually put that knowledge to good use.

How many brilliant, but utterly clueless people do you know? They may have a PhD, but they don't have the slightest idea how to make it in life. They have their heads full of knowledge, but they don't have even a modicum of understanding. They have vast stores of facts—but those facts are very nearly worthless because they are simply not functional.

This equates to a kind of "educational autism," of which my wife and I are painfully aware, and to which I will speak later in this chapter. Autistic individuals may be able to memorize an entire encyclopedia but be unable to reason their way through a simple decision about which shoe to put on first. They are full of facts but unable to function—essentially paralyzed—which keeps them from leaving the room to share their "knowledge." They have been educated beyond their intelligence. A fellow eastern Kentuckian said it this way: "When you got no education, you just have to use your brains."

Understanding is making connections between all the facts. It is what makes knowledge useful. It is what makes knowledge practical. It is what makes knowledge functional. It is what takes the ABCs of math or science or literature and translates them into real life. It applies knowledge. It puts knowledge in a context. It makes knowledge relevant.

Wisdom is the most practical—but often the least developed—of educational attributes. It is what allows knowledge and understanding to actually go to work in the world. Wisdom is discernment. Wisdom is discretion. Wisdom is differentiation. It takes knowledge out of the ivory tower and engages it down where the rubber meets the road. Wisdom unleashes understanding, turns it loose on the hurly-burly world of conflicting facts, contradictory evidence, and contrarian notions. Wisdom integrates knowledge and makes it more than just a jumble of data.

To knowledge is added understanding; to understanding is added wisdom; and then, and only then, may truth be attained.

If any of us is ever to be successful in this life, we need to know not only "what" but "why" as well. We not only need to know "who," "where," and "when," but we also need to know "how." When we begin to understand an issue, a question, a dilemma, a principle, or an idea, then and only then can we move beyond our current state of sloppy thinking and sloppy living.

The problem with all of this, of course, is that it is fairly easy to teach the basic facts of a subject—that process is essentially a one-way street. It is much harder to teach for understanding—because that process is essentially a two-way street and thus much more complicated. It cannot be reduced to mere formulas. It cannot be contained in curriculum standards. It cannot be programmed. It requires personal attention and investment. It demands mentoring, modeling, and motivating—and often that is only possible one-on-one. Wisdom is even more difficult to arrive at—and it is not particularly cost effective; it is terribly inefficient. But such is the path to truth.

Besides all that, grappling with wisdom and truth can be dangerous—it involves value judgments. And value judgments involve values. In other words, the pathway to true education is not ethically neutral. Truth takes a stand. Justice may be blind, but wisdom is anything but blind. Indeed, it is searchingly astute.

Wisdom is alert, penetrating, discerning, and vigilant. Truth is a sentinel watching out over the field of danger. Wisdom is a herald shouting out through the din of the throng. Truth is a searchlight shining through the fog of confusion. Wisdom is clarity, precision, insight, and focus. Truth is sharp, certain, and unhesitating. Wisdom is rare but indispensable. Truth is scarce but essential. Wisdom is uncommon but vital. Truth is the object—the only object—of education.

Wisdom and truth are the only things that can insure that the great legacy of freedom, the inheritance of cultural greatness, and the blessings of progress will continue. Thus, they are worth every risk. They are worth every expense.

EDUCATING FOR WISDOM AND TRUTH

According to a *Forbes* magazine profile, the National Education Association (NEA) is "the worm in the American education apple."[36] The normally sedate business journal went on to say, "The public may be only dimly aware of it, but the union's growing power has exactly coincided with the dismal spectacle of rising spending on education producing deteriorating results."[37] Syndicated columnist James Kilpatrick agrees. He wrote, "The NEA in recent years has come to embody every single cause that has contributed to the crisis that threatens our public schools."[38]

Founded in 1857 by representatives of several state teachers associations, the National Education Association is today the country's largest labor union. With a membership now approaching three million, an annual combined budget of $500 million, and a standing political war chest of nearly $20 million, the union is one of the most powerful forces in American life today.[39] It is the largest single interest group lobbying in Washington.[40] It has the largest and richest political action committee.[41] It is the biggest broker of group insurance benefits.[42] And it is the major ideological force in more than 90 percent of the some sixteen thousand local public school districts throughout the nation.[43]

For nearly thirty years, the union has maintained a smothering monopoly over every aspect of America's government-run educational system—from the content of the curriculum to the proposal of budgets, from the design of facilities to the administration of bureaucracies, from classroom methodologies to teacher salaries, from political reform to regulatory control.[44]

But its appetite for new kingdoms to conquer remains unsatisfied. According to author and educator Phoebe Courtney, the union is not satisfied simply controlling public education. "It wants complete control over all American education—private as well as public. It has vowed to bring private education under its control through teacher certification and state accreditation laws."[45]

To that end, the union has launched a series of initiatives aimed at consolidating its power nationwide:

- It has worked diligently to promote the nationalization of educational standards—to insure complete uniformity in teaching content, methodology, administration, and outcome.[46]

- It has spent millions of dollars fighting against school choice measures that would allow parents to choose the best schooling options for their children according to their own criteria.[47]

- It has fought for either the elimination or the strict regulation of homeschooling—in some states even going so far as to establish "enforcement units" to identify and seek prosecution of parents that homeschool their children without government approval or certification.[48]

- It has attempted to stymie any and all educational reform—particularly when that reform has involved diversifying the educational options available to taxpayers and parents.[49]

- It has lobbied for centralization of control of the financing of education—recommending that the current system of local financing be scrapped for a federal system.[50]

In 1967, Sam Lambert, the union's executive secretary, predicted, "The National Education Association will become a political power second to no other special interest group.... We will organize this profession from top to bottom into logical operational units that can move swiftly and effectively and with power unmatched by any other organized group in the nation."[51]

By all counts, that prophecy has been fulfilled. But the standards of education have only worsened.

As if to add insult to injury, the NEA has even fought against such educational reform efforts as the "No Child Left Behind" measures. It has organized resistance to parental and community involvement at every turn. And amazingly, this massive, radical, and reactionary teacher's union has been able to continue to be the most influential force in American education today—more influential even than the combined strength of the White House and both houses of Congress.

Clearly, to restore wisdom and truth to our nation's schools and to our children's lives will require far more of us than simply another flurry of reformist legislation from the educational elite in the National Education Association. It will require more than simply additional recommendations on interactive media, computer software technology enhancements, comprehensive correlative curricula, outcome-based objectives, trade affinity matrices, life skills development, and turnkey textual exercises. Not only will the NEA have to be put in its place, but also a whole new commitment to understanding and wisdom will have to be emphasized. Not only will the NEA have to be removed from its privileged cultural pedestal, but also the great legacy of Christendom will have to be recovered.

The brilliant men and women who wove the fabric of Western civilization and left us a legacy of freedom and opportunity knew nothing of "correlative curricula or programmed outcomes or software enhancements"—but they were *educated*. And they were educated in a way that we can only dream of today despite all our nifty gadgets, gimmicks, and bright ideas. They thus were able to preserve and then to pass on to their progeny a heritage of real substance. It is that kind of education we must begin to restore if we are to have any hope of preserving a culture of moral clarity.

CREATING ALTERNATIVES

Several years ago, I was visiting a public school library in order to film a segment for a television program. While I was waiting for a technical problem to be resolved, I went to the bookshelves and casually picked up the first book my eyes happened to rest upon. I opened the book, not looking for anything in particular, and began to read. I was astounded. "So you're pregnant," the book declared. "Your parents have an opinion. Your teachers have an opinion. Your pastor or priest has an opinion. But the only opinion that really matters is yours." I was shocked. I had known for quite some time that it was essential that parents who want their children educated without that kind of undermining of authority seek out alternatives. The incident reinforced my conviction that parents need to be empowered to make good educational decisions for their children.

The problem is money.

In my home state of Ohio, local school districts depend on two primary means of funding. One is aid directly from the state government, and the second is personal property taxes. Money for education has been an issue for as long as I can remember.

When I was a high school student, I attended what was known as split sessions for one school year while my school district was building a larger high school to accommodate rapid growth in our community. State aid alone was never enough, so taxpayers were asked to approve additional tax levies on their homes to generate money for building projects.

In 1973, a ballot initiative called *State Issue 1* was put before voters in the general election in Ohio. If passed, this issue would create a state lottery commission; it was approved by a two-to-one margin. The number one selling point by backers of this issue was that the revenue generated would go to the schools. The lottery actually began in August 1974. It was not until July 1983, however, that the state legislature earmarked lottery profits for education, and it was not until November 1987 that voters, in another statewide initiative, approved a constitutional amendment to permanently earmark lottery profits for education.

Since its inception in 1974, the lottery has contributed more than $13 billion to education in Ohio. When divided by thirty years and more than six hundred school districts, that figure amounts to a fraction of what an individual school district needs. In 2003, the payment to education was less than one-third of the lottery's total ticket sales. This is just another example of secular government thinking that money is the answer to all ills. School funding in Ohio has been in crisis for the past several years—as it has been in most other sections of the country. But money alone won't fix this fundamentally flawed system.

What if a small portion of education funding was made available in the form of vouchers? Two things would happen immediately. One, public schools would lose their monopoly on education and be forced to perform in a competitive atmosphere. Two, parents would have a multitude of options from which to choose when deciding how their children should be educated. In the end, everyone would benefit.

One of the chief arguments against school vouchers and opening up competition between the public and private sectors in education is that children with special needs and children from poor families will simply be left behind. I know from the experience of my own family that need not be the case.

Our son Austin has gone to Harvest Preparatory School, established as an educational branch of our ministry several years ago, ever since he was in the first grade. In many ways, that is a miracle in and of itself.

I doubt if there is anything more difficult for parents than watching their children struggle. When Austin was diagnosed at age three with a form of autism called *Asperger's Syndrome*, we began a quest simply to help him function each day. The pain for us was not in the process or in the pursuit of treatment but in watching our beautiful child struggle while we couldn't "make it all better."

"No hope, no cure, no treatment." I will never forget the day the doctor gave us that prognosis. That statement changed our lives forever. At the time, it almost seemed as if a death sentence had been pronounced, but it was really just another way of starting us on an amazing journey. Instead of "no hope, no cure, no treatment," God was saying, "On your mark, get set, go!"

Through the prayer and persistence of faithful teachers and friends, Austin progressed and, amazingly, left his silent world and began to speak and later communicate. He now goes to our school. He has friends, laughs, and enjoys life. He has met and conquered so many challenges and has been the biggest life lesson and example to our family.

He continues to have some struggles, which are, quite honestly, the source of daily heartbreak. There are still unanswered questions, still unsolved mysteries where this disorder is concerned and how it affects so many children and families. However, we have chosen to embrace the positive, the gift that is our son, knowing that faith in God turns tragedy into triumph.

We have seen the beauty, comfort, and diligent faithfulness that education can be—when it is something more than just the pursuit of knowledge. When it is a life integration of understanding and wisdom, when it is a pursuit of truth, lives are changed. Certainly, ours have been.

THE TRUTH WILL SET US FREE

Unhampered and unfettered truth is the only ground upon which honest, open, and free relationships may be built—whether in families and communities or among societies and nations. Wisdom, as it has been expressed through all the ages, has always welcomed the truth, the whole truth, and nothing but the truth. That is why education—education that is more than just a pursuit of knowledge—is so important.

In order to advance the cause of life and liberty in these difficult days, we will have to recover what we have lost. The kind of education our Founding Fathers enjoyed, the kind of education that made our nation the envy of the world, and the kind of education that gave us the statesmen and geniuses and heroes of the past can be our greatest gift to the next generation. But only if we have the will and the confidence that truth will indeed bear its cherished fruit.

The American experiment in liberty was rooted in that kind of confidence. And if the experiment is to continue in the days ahead—benefiting our children, grandchildren, and great-grandchildren—then we must take care to follow in their footsteps.

There is no need for us to attempt to reinvent the wheel. The battle for truth has been fought again and again and again—successfully. We need not cast about for direction. We need not grope in the dark for strategies, programs, and agendas. We need not manufacture new ideas, new priorities, or new tactics. We already have a tested and proven formula for victory. We already have a winning legacy. We simply need to reclaim it. We simply need to recover what is rightfully ours. Whatever the cost, we need only to rely upon the truth.

The infamous skeptic Friedrich Nietzsche once confessed, "We all fear truth."[52] Why would he say that? Because, as the great Spanish author Cervantes asserted, "Truth may be stretched, but it cannot be broken, and always gets above falsehood, as oil does above water."[53] That is a fearsome thing to doubters. On the other hand, it is a great relief to all the rest of us.

As Emily Dickinson beautifully conveyed in one of her most eloquent poems:

> Opinion is a flitting thing,
> But Truth, outlasts the Sun;
> If then we cannot own them both,
> Possess the oldest one.

After all, it is the truth that will ultimately set us free.[54]

ACTION POINTS

- Support private education efforts in areas where they are available.

- If private education is not available in your area, get involved in the education process by:
  — Finding out about curriculum
  — Supporting school board candidates who have moral views
  — Talking to your children about what they are learning

- Work for the implementation of a school choice voucher system.

- Recommended reading:
  Grading the NEA, by Perry L. Glanzer, PhD, and Travis Pardo[55]

  NEA: Trojan Horse in American Education, by Samuel Blumenfeld[56]

CHAPTER 7

LIFE:
Inalienable Rights, Irreplaceable People
SILENT NO MORE

> We hold these truths to be self-evident: that all men
> are created equal, that they are endowed by their
> Creator with certain unalienable rights, that among
> these are life, liberty, and the pursuit of happiness.
>
> —THOMAS JEFFERSON

Is there any subject that is more controversial? Is there any topic, any debate, any issue that can so quickly divide? Is there any discussion that can so easily polarize families, communities, and nations? Is it even conceivable that there is a hotter hot-button issue anywhere? If there is, I can't think of what it might be.

Abortion is one of those watershed issues that seem to cut a wide swath of division right through the whole host of mankind. President Ronald Reagan went so far as to call it the "defining issue of our age." But then, so did Senator Hillary Clinton. And as you might have guessed, the two were on opposite ends of the question.

It is certainly easy to see why abortion elicits such adamant opposing responses. The questions of life and choice, of law and freedom, of medical technology and civil morality, of private liberty and public responsibility are all vitally important—and abortion has an extraordinary impact upon each of those questions. But the real reason abortion is such a divisive and polarizing issue is that in the end we cannot get away from the fundamental principle that people matter. Instinctively we know that every life is worth affirming, enabling, and protecting.

Whenever a crisis occurs, what do we think about? What is our immediate reaction? Our first concern is for the people involved, of course. What happened? Is everyone all right? Was anybody hurt? Did help arrive in time? Is there anything we can do?

It doesn't really matter whether the crisis is a natural disaster or a terrorist attack. It isn't particularly important whether it is an accident or a crime. It makes no real difference whether it is a national calamity or a personal tragedy. Our first thought is always of the people, isn't it?

If a tornado devastates an entire community, but everyone is somehow able to safely ride out the storm, we invariably breathe a sigh of relief. Even if they have lost everything they own, we will say, "At least no one was hurt. That is the most important thing." Indeed, it is the most important thing. People matter. They matter more than anything else. Of that we are certain.

If our child is involved in a car wreck, the first thing we want to know is if our child is going to be OK. At that moment, we are not really interested in the damage to the vehicle, what happened in the intersection, or where the fault lies—not until we hear a voice on the other end of the phone say, "I'm fine, Mom. Really, I got out without a scratch. Don't worry." In moments like that, our priorities are crystal clear. It is the people who matter.

When we hear about an explosion at a factory, if we see a report of a crime wave on the evening news, or if we get a message about an epidemic of the flu, we immediately fire off the e-mails and phone calls to check on the people we care about. We will drop everything without a moment's hesitation to find out how they are doing. We care. We care because people matter. People matter more anything else.

Whether they are on the battlefield or on the highway, out in the suburbs or in the inner city, at home or far, far away, we acknowledge in large and small ways every day that people are precious. Their lives are of inestimable value. They are gifts. They must never be taken for granted. Things can be replaced—but there is no replacement for a mother, father, sister, brother, aunt, uncle, friend, or neighbor.

Civil societies always recognize this vital principle, and they build their cultural institutions upon it. They will do anything and everything they possibly can to protect the dignity, integrity, and sanctity of life. Because there are no expendable or disposable people, every life is worth honoring, protecting, and saving. Ultimately, the rule of law depends upon an absolute respect for the value of people as people and not as property.

LAW, LIFE, AND LIBERTY

The founders of the great American experiment in liberty understood that principle only too well. They staked their lives, their fortunes, and their sacred honor on the proposition that freedom could only be secured against the arbitrary whims of men and movements by the rule of law. The American system of government, therefore, has never depended upon the good will of politicians, the charity of the rich, or the wisdom of the powerful. Instead, every single citizen, regardless of his or her station, education, or vocation, has been considered equal under the standard of unchanging, immutable, and impartial justice. Everyone was to be treated equally because everyone mattered equally.

Thomas Paine stated this principle in *Common Sense*, the powerful little booklet that helped spark the War for Independence. "In America," he said, "the law is king."[1] The rule of law was so important to the founders because they understood that even the best political policies and principles, when left to the care of mere human authorities, all too easily devolve into tyranny. Even when entrusted to the will of the 51 percent, our most sacred ideals can erode over time. By the end of the eighteenth century, history was already replete with examples of the very best of intentions shipwrecked on the shifting shoals of subjectivity. Thus, the founders understood that there had to be some kind of an absolute with which prejudice or preference could never interfere. They knew they had to lay a foundation for freedom that the winds of change and the waters of circumstance could not erode. They knew that there had to be an objective basis for law that could be depended upon at all times, in all places, and in every situation. It would be this remarkable Christian innovation in the affairs of men and nations that would set America apart from every would-be utopia of opportunity and every should-have-been refuge of freedom.

It should not be surprising, then, that the opening refrain of the Declaration of Independence would emphasize this very truth. Thus, the famous words of Thomas Jefferson clearly affirmed the necessity of an absolute standard upon which the rule of law would have to be based: "We hold these truths to be self-evident, that all men are created equal; that they are endowed by their Creator with certain inalienable rights; that among these are life, liberty, and the pursuit of happiness. That, to secure these rights, governments are instituted among men, deriving their just powers from the consent of the governed."[2]

This did not mean that Jefferson and the other founders believed that all men actually were equal—in ability, in station, or even in opportunity. They were idealists, but they were not unrealistic idealists. They were only too well aware of the fact that we live in a very diverse and fallen world where the differences between us are all too obvious, and the violations of justice are all too frequent. Rather, it meant that they were committed to making the guiding principle of the new nation the equal value of every single life, every single citizen, and every single person.

Appealing to the "Supreme Judge of the World" for guidance, and relying on His "Divine Providence" for wisdom, the Founding Fathers committed themselves and their posterity to the absolute standard of "the laws of nature and nature's God." And the essence of that standard, they said, was the inalienable, God-given, and sovereignly endowed rights of life, liberty, and the pursuit of happiness. A "just government exists," they argued, solely and completely to "provide guards" for the "future security" of that essence. Take that away, and not only is sure and secure justice no longer possible, but the rule of law is no longer possible either.[3]

Thomas Jefferson would later reinforce that conviction, saying, "The chief purpose of government is to protect life. Abandon that, and you have abandoned all."[4]

Abraham Lincoln questioned the legitimacy of chattel slavery along the same lines. The "peculiar institution" was a threat to the rule of law, he argued, precisely because it was a denial of the sanctity of all human life. "I should like to know if taking this old Declaration of Independence, which declares that all men are equal upon principle, and making exceptions to it, where it will stop. If one man says it does not mean a Negro, why not another say it does not mean some other man?"[5]

The statesmen and heroes of the American republic have always understood that whenever the principle of the dignity and sanctity of life is questioned, the rule of law is automatically thrown into very real jeopardy. No one, then, is absolutely secure, because absoluteness will have been thrown out of the constitutional vocabulary. When the right to life is abrogated for at least some citizens, all the liberties of all the citizens are at risk, because suddenly arbitrariness, relativism, and randomness have entered into the legal equation.

That is why the struggle for the abolition of the slave trade, the emancipation of the slaves, and the guarantee of their civil rights afterward were such a test of the genuineness of the American constitutional vision. At stake was not simply the dignity, integrity, and sanctity of the lives of African Americans—it was not just their rights that were threatened. At stake was the entire American vision, because suddenly we were confronted by an exception to the principle that people matter—indeed, that all people matter. Left unchecked, the slavery of the few would have meant slavery for the many.

Thomas Jefferson even acknowledged as much, saying:

> Can the liberties of a nation be sure when we re-
> move their only firm basis, a conviction in the
> minds of the people, that these liberties are the gift
> of God? That they are not to be violated but with
> His wrath? Indeed, I tremble for my country, when
> I reflect that God is just; that His justice cannot
> sleep forever, that revolution of the wheel of fortune,
> a change of situation, is among possible events; that
> it may become probable by supernatural influence!
> The Almighty has no attribute which can take side
> with us in that event.[6]

Because Americans built their culture on the principle that people matter more than any other expediency, any other convenience, or any other right, we became known around the world not only for our laws, which insured liberty, but also for our character, which insured greatness.

Because we have always believed that people matter more than anything else, not only did our culture protect the dignity, integrity, and sanctity of life, but also we respected it. The entire structure of liberty rested on this foundation.

Now, at this point you are probably asking yourself, "If the protection of life is so essential to the maintenance of freedom and is so integral to any good and decent society, why is abortion an issue at all?" If you are not asking that question, you should be. The sanctity of life is one of those central truths that the Founding Fathers thought to be "self-evident" in the sense that it is written on the fleshly tablet of every man's heart. How could something so vital and so obvious have ever become so controversial and so disputed? How is it possible that the principle of the value of every single life has actually divided us as a people and a nation?

Certainly it is not because some advocates of abortion still claim that children in the womb are just "blobs of tissue." Even the most radical proabortion activist no longer argues that. Science has demonstrated beyond any shadow of a doubt that a fetus is fully human from the moment of conception. Have you seen the fabulous *in utero* photography and ultrasound images that modern medical advances have been able to produce? They are breathtaking. No, there is no question about whether the victims of abortion are actually people.

So why is abortion still an option? Why have the courts decided to give one group of people the choice, the right, to snuff out the lives of another group of people? How is it that we have come to accept the fact that almost every third baby conceived in America is killed by abortion? How could we possibly have gotten to the place where 43 percent of American women undergo at least one abortion during their childbearing years?

There are at least two answers to these questions. One has to do with a progressive numbing of our society's moral clarity. The other has to do with money and power. Both answers ought to be very disturbing to us all.

BARBARIZATION

While life may be essential to the maintenance of freedom, you would hardly know it by looking at our current popular culture. Over the course of the past several decades, we have seen the American commitment to life and liberty under assault by a whole host of dangerous trends. These trends have in many ways depersonalized what was once a very personable culture. Disrespect has become rampant. Incivility is more and more common. We are often rude and crude to one another, mocking and disrespectful to authority, and irreverent and contemptuous to time-honored convention. As Mike Huckabee, governor of Arkansas, has argued, "We are inclined to laud renegades, rebels, and antiheroes as celebrities, icons, and role models."[7]

As a result of our embrace of Hollywood's "sex, drugs, and rock and roll" mind-set, it has been easier for us to dismiss the value of one another and to play into the hand of an increasingly violent, sullen, and perverse countercultural backlash.

According to many criminal investigators, the first and most important factor in stripping away inhibitions against crime—including rape and murder—is the ability to depersonalize the victim. A criminal predator needs to distance himself psychologically from his victim's humanity. His disrespect for the possessions or the life of his target depends upon his ability to ignore or deny personal integrity or sanctity. He needs to justify his actions by redefining his prey as a mere "thing."

Lt. Col. Dave Grossman is an expert in the area of cultural violence. He has argued that "killers are made, not born." Thus, according to Grossman, "In World War II, only 15 to 20 percent of combat infantry were actually willing to fire their rifles; in Korea, about 50 percent were; in Vietnam, the figure rose to over 90 percent."[8] What made the difference? According to Grossman, it was the training they received. Military theorists and strategists began to explore different methods in an effort to help soldiers overcome their "powerful, innate human resistance" to killing.[9] They began to put in place certain exercises that would enable soldiers to psychologically depersonalize the enemy.[10] Without that kind of conditioning, most men are naturally "contentious objectors" on the battlefield.[11]

Perhaps not surprisingly, the same ideas apply to societies. In order for cultures to become violent, barbaric, and uncaring, they have to be trained to be violent, barbaric, and uncaring. According to Grossman, our natural inhibitions against criminal assault are strong. Thus, without careful conditioning, most people are simply incapable of hurting, much less killing, another human being. Except in cases of extreme emotional trauma, we all have a natural psychological resistance to murder. In order to actually pull a trigger or lunge with a knife, we have to first systematically desensitize our innate sense of the sanctity of another person's life.

Alas, we have worked very hard, it seems, to do just that to ourselves and to our children. We have set into motion societal trends that break down our natural inhibitions against depersonalizing people. Already numbed by the violence-saturated video games, movies, music, Web sites, and television, our sensitivity to the value of life has been eroded even more by our legal and institutional commitment to death—abortion, infanticide, and euthanasia. We have begun the process of redefining whole categories of people as "things." In the media, in sex-education literature, in political discourse, and in the arrangements of daily life, we have begun to diminish the personhood of us all by diminishing the personhood of a few.

Consider, for instance, how the debate over the brutal partial-birth abortion procedure has taken us far down the road to depersonalization. According to Robert Bork:

> These abortions are performed very late in the pregnancy. The baby is delivered feet first until only the head remains within the mother. The aborting physician inserts scissors into the back of the infant's skull and opens the blades to produce a hole. The child's brains are then vacuumed out, the skull collapses, and the rest of the newly made corpse is removed. If the head had been allowed to come out of the mother, killing the baby, then would be the criminal act of infanticide. When it was proposed to outlaw this hideous procedure, which obviously causes extreme pain to the baby, the proabortion forces in Congress and elsewhere made false statements to fend off the legislation or to justify an anticipated presidential veto. Planned Parenthood stated that the general anesthesia given to the mother killed the fetus so that there was no such thing as a partial birth abortion. Physicians promptly rebutted the claim. Local anesthesia, which is most often used in these abortions, has no effect on the baby, and general anesthesia not only does not kill the baby, it provides little or no painkilling effect to the baby. Two doctors who perform partial birth abortions admitted that the

majority of fetuses aborted in this fashion are alive until the end of the procedure.[12]

Thus, Bork concluded:

> Other opponents of a ban on partial birth abortions claimed that it was used only when necessary to protect the mother's life. Unfortunately for that argument, the physician who is the best-known practitioner of these abortions stated that 80 percent of them are purely elective, not necessary to save the mother's life or health. Partial birth underscores the matter. The baby is outside the mother except for its head, which is kept in the mother only to avoid the charge of infanticide. Full birth is inches away and could easily be accomplished.[13]

It is difficult to see how anyone can fail to understand how a culture that justifies, defends, and institutionalizes such barbarism is in serious jeopardy of stripping away our natural inhibitions against killing in other arenas and spheres. Now we have begun to think what was once unthinkable. We are excusing what was once inexcusable. We have made a matter of conscience what was once unconscionable. Those charged with protecting and preserving life are now engaged in assaulting and taking it.

Court precedents for abortion have recently been recycled for the causes of euthanasia, assisted suicide, and mercy killing.[14] As Bork has convincingly argued, "Decisions about life and death in one area influence such decisions in others. Despite assurances that the abortion decisions did not start us down a slippery and very steep slope, that is clearly where we are, and gathering speed."[15]

At every turn human life is loudly and legally devalued. The sick, the elderly, the unborn, the unwanted, the disabled, the despised, and the rejected have become little more than the discarded refuse of our mad rush for self-fulfillment and self-satisfaction.

That we are appalled by the effects of our actions but continue to approve of their genesis demonstrates extreme myopia. There can be no divorce of fruit from root.

If we are ever to regain our equilibrium as a society, if we are to rescue our children from a downward spiral of violence, then we must recover our founding ideals. We must resensitize ourselves to the dignity, integrity, and sanctity of life by upholding it at every opportunity and in every situation. People matter.

THE DEATH INDUSTRY

While all these cultural trends seem to have allowed and even promoted abortion on demand, in the end it is money that has made abortion such a sacred cow in modern America. The fact is that abortion is big business. There is a great deal of money at stake in maintaining the current course of legal child killing. In fact, there is a multibillion-dollar-a-year industry that depends on continuing this dangerous erosion of the sanctity of life.

Take the example of Planned Parenthood, for instance. The organization is command central for the burgeoning abortion industry.[16] Along with the National Organization for Women (NOW) and the National Abortion Rights Action League (NARAL), Planned Parenthood has done more to sway American culture away from its commitment to "life, liberty, and the pursuit of happiness" than any other organization, movement, or trend. As you will soon see, it is one of the most potent forces for the modern liberal agenda anywhere, from any time in all of history.

According to George Grant's definitive book on the subject, "Planned Parenthood is the world's oldest, largest, and best-organized provider of abortion and birth control services."[17] The organization began just over seventy years ago in a two-room makeshift clinic in a rundown Brooklyn neighborhood, staffed by three untrained but radical volunteers.[18] But it has now grown into a multibillion-dollar international conglomerate with programs and activities in hundreds of nations on every continent.[19]

In the United States alone, it employs more than twenty thousand staff personnel and volunteers in nearly a thousand clinics and almost two hundred affiliates in every major metropolitan area, coast to coast. The organization boasts a national office in New York, a legislative center in Washington, regional offices in Atlanta, Chicago, Miami, and San Francisco, and international offices in London, Nairobi, Bangkok, and New Delhi. All in all, the Federation has posted more than $25 million in earnings annually for the last decade with hundreds of millions in cash reserves and hundreds of millions more in capital assets. With estimated combined annual budgets—including all the various regional and international service affiliates—of more than a trillion dollars, Planned Parenthood may very well be the largest and most profitable nonprofit organization in history.[20]

No wonder the abortion industry is so well protected and organized. And no wonder it is so vital to its interests to keep the grisly procedure legal through all nine months of pregnancy.

Planned Parenthood has used its considerable wealth, manpower, and influence to muscle its way into virtually every aspect of modern life.[21] According to Grant:

It now plays a strategic role in the health and social services community—and plans to figure prominently in any future health care reform plan. It exerts a major influence on education—providing the majority of sex-education curricula and programs in both public and private schools. It carries considerable political clout through lobbying, legislation, campaigning, advocacy, and litigation—coordinating the substantial efforts of the rest of the multibillion-dollar abortion industry. It is involved in publishing, broadcast media production, judicial activism, public relations, foreign aid, psychological research, counseling, contraceptive distribution and sales, mass advertising, and public legal service provision.[22]

You name it, and Planned Parenthood does it. The organization is like a multinational corporate conglomerate, dedicated to spreading the proabortion message and lifestyle as far and as wide as it possibly can.

The organization is practically a "Teflon cultural icon." It has gained all of its great influence, power, and wealth despite the fact that the organization has been belligerently controversial from its earliest days. It has used its considerable political heft, its seemingly bottomless public relations war chest, its enormous prestige, and its "benign, American-as-apple-pie name"[23] in an effort to steer our culture as close to the brink of total radicalism as possible. The organization actually began as a part of the Greenwich Village communist cabal during the years just after the First World War. It eventually allied itself with such fringe movements as Eugenics and National Socialism. It has invariably tinkered with bad politics and bad science.

As a result, through the years it has had to fight off the outrage of parents who were shocked at the promiscuous content of the organization's sex-education materials.[24] Consumer boycotts have begun to jeopardize its lucrative corporate philanthropy program.[25] Tough questions about its militantly partisan programs have threatened its nonprofit status.[26] Disclosure demands over the organization's burgeoning profits from contraceptive sales have put a damper on its marketing campaigns.[27] In addition, a spate of medical malpractice lawsuits from botched abortions has intensified the organization's already looming insurability crisis.[28] The stigmatization of grisly child-killing abortion procedures has dramatically reduced the number of physicians willing to perform them. As a result, Planned Parenthood clinics have been forced to rely on less adequately trained personnel—nurse practitioners and doctors who have failed in private or institutional practices.[29] Revelations about deliberately suppressed research data on abortion risks—particularly concerning the established links between abortion and breast cancer—have raised new questions about the organization's medical objectivity and professional integrity.[30]

But despite all this, the huge Planned Parenthood juggernaut seems just to roll along. According to syndicated columnist Cal Thomas, "Planned Parenthood has enjoyed one of the longest free rides in political history."[31] In fact, according to a recent annual report, "While some might think that controversy necessarily results in decreased support, Planned Parenthood has found the opposite to be true."[32]

The real problem with Planned Parenthood, though, is not simply that the organization has used its vast resources to pursue its radical agenda at the public's expense. That is certainly troubling. The real problem is that the organization endangers lives and health at every turn. Its blind commitment to growing the death industry has made its well-heeled, taxpayer-supported programs a real threat to women, their children, and their families.

Planned Parenthood's program of birth control, for instance, has not only failed to inhibit unwanted pregnancies, but it has also increased the risk of severe medical problems for the women who follow it. In fact, the Planned Parenthood system virtually guarantees that women will get pregnant—and that they will then be "forced" to fall back on the birth control linchpin: abortion. Safe and effective? Not by a long shot.

Planned Parenthood's battle against sexually transmitted diseases is also a dismal failure. In fact, the organization's efforts have been tragically counterproductive. It has become a veritable Typhoid Mary, actually encouraging the spread of syphilis, gonorrhea, chlamydia, herpes, hepatitis, granuloma, chancroid, and even AIDS at an alarming rate. Besides the fact that it constantly exhorts youngsters to flaunt promiscuity, it continually promotes an alarmingly "unsafe" exercise of that promiscuity. "Apparently," says demographic analyst Robert Ruff, "Planned Parenthood believes that safe sex is a lot less important than free sex."[33]

Even the organization's multimillion-dollar, tax-funded education programs threaten the lives and health of women and their children. According to its own survey, conducted by the Louis Harris pollsters, teens who have taken their "comprehensive" sex-education courses have a 50 percent higher rate of sexual activity than their unenlightened peers.[34] And yet, the courses had no significant effect on their contraceptive usage.[35] The conclusion, one that even Planned Parenthood researchers have been unable to escape, is that their sex-education courses only exacerbate the teen pregnancy problem.[36]

In 1970, fewer than half of the nation's school districts offered sex-education curricula, and none had school-based birth control clinics.[37] Today, more than 75 percent of the districts teach sex education, and there are more than three hundred clinics in operation.[38] Yet the percentage of illegitimate births has only increased during that time, from a mere 15 percent to an astonishing 51 percent.[39] According to the Harris poll, the only things that effectively impact the teen pregnancy problem are frequent church attendance and parental oversight—the very things that sex-education courses are designed to circumvent.[40]

Planned Parenthood's influential and expensive programs have not only failed to address the problems they were supposed to solve, but they have also made them worse. The cure has been worse than the disease. Here is an organization that has done more than any other to make abortion on demand through all nine months of pregnancy the law of the land. Not only have they made it the law of the land, but they have also made it an unquestioned part of our lives and our culture. And the results have been disastrous in every way imaginable.

Nevertheless, this is the organization that has been sitting in the cultural driver's seat. Consider the fact that according to some estimates, as many as one out of every six abortions today is performed on a woman who identifies herself as a "born-again Christian." With some 1.5 million abortions performed each year, this means that perhaps as many as 250,000 evangelical Christians are aborting their children every year. It appears that the influence of Planned Parenthood's worldview is greater for these women than the worldview of the Bible.

Likewise, minority women have accepted the distorted logic of Planned Parenthood in disproportionate numbers, and the results have been devastating. African Americans make up only 14 percent of women of childbearing age in America, but they account for more than 31 percent of all abortions. Hispanic women constitute 10.6 percent of this same group but suffer more than 20 percent of the total abortions in America. Together, these two minority groups account for less than 25 percent of women of childbearing age in America, but they account for more than half of the total babies aborted in the country. In other words, minority women are aborting at more than twice the rate of white women.[41]

The fact is that more African American babies have been killed by abortion during the last quarter century than the total number of African American deaths from all other causes combined. The statistics are horrifying: 203,695 from AIDS, 306,313 from violent crimes, 370,723 from accidents, 1,638,350 from cancer, and 2,266,789 from heart disease. The number from abortion? More than 13 million![42] In almost any other context this would have to be considered racial genocide. Alas, in America it is just "freedom of choice."

A TERRIBLE LOSS

Who can possibly calculate the loss to our culture, to our economy, and to our history caused by our cavalier approach to life? The logic of abortion is devastating. Just consider the consequences to history if Planned Parenthood had always had its way.

How would abortion advocates have counseled this family, for instance? A preacher and his wife have fourteen children. They are already living in abject poverty when she discovers that she is pregnant again. Should she abort for the good of the rest of her family?

Or consider another case: A father is chronically ill with bronchitis, and his wife has tuberculosis. They have already had four children. The first is blind, the second died in infancy, the third is deaf, and the fourth has tuberculosis. Then she discovers that she is once again pregnant. Should she abort and save everyone from further misery?

Or consider this case: A white man raped a thirteen-year-old black girl. She became pregnant. Should her worried parents spare her the trauma and stigma of carrying the child to term?

Or yet another case: A teenage girl is pregnant. Though she is not married, she is engaged. Her fiancé is not the father of the baby, and naturally he's very upset. Would you consider recommending abortion in this very complicated situation?

If you answered yes to any of these situations, you just recommended the elimination of John Wesley, one of the greatest reformers and evangelists of the eighteenth century; Ludwig von Beethoven, one of the greatest composers of the nineteenth century; Ethel Waters, one of the greatest jazz and gospel musicians of the twentieth century; and finally, the Lord Jesus Christ. At what cost to life, liberty, and human society do we continue to give ourselves over to the logic of Planned Parenthood and the death industry?

A WAY FORWARD

As Alan Keyes has so eloquently asserted:

> America has once again arrived at a momentous crossroads. We are going to have to decide—as we have had to decide so many times in the past— whether we shall only *speak* of justice and *speak* of principle, or whether we shall *stand* and *fight* for them. We are going to have to decide whether we shall quote the words of the Declaration of Independence with real conviction, or whether we shall

take that document and throw it on the ash heap of history as we adopt the message of those who insist that we stand silent in the face of injustice. When it comes to deciding whether we shall stand by the great principle that declares that all human beings are "created equal" and "endowed by their Creator" with the "right to life," it seems to me, there is no choice for silence.[43]

In order to protect and preserve any rights, courageous leaders—in the press, in medicine, in law, in politics, and in the church—have always recognized that they had to protect and preserve all the rights of all the people, beginning with the fundamental rights of life, liberty, and the pursuit of happiness. They had to match the rhetoric of liberty with the activity of liberation.

We certainly can do no less in these difficult days in which we live.

ACTION POINTS

- Volunteer at and support your local crisis pregnancy center or resource center.

- Visit www.operationoutcry.org, which is especially helpful for those needing postabortive healing and restoration.

- Visit www.thinkaboutitonline.com for additional information about abortion and the abortion industry.

- Investigate what your local school is doing to teach abstinence to teens. Work within the school district to have abstinence-only sex-education curriculum beginning in the fifth grade.

- Recommended reading:

Parents, Teens and Sex: The Big Talk Book, by
Bruce Cook—helpful information about talking to your children about sex and sexuality[44]

Answering the Call, by John Ensor—reading
for pastors and church leaders[45]

Prolife Answers to Prochoice Arguments, by
Randy Alcorn[46]

*Grand Illusions: The Legacy of Planned
Parenthood*, by George Grant[47]

For a way to weave the message of justice and
mercy, as they relate to the issue of the sanctity
of life, into the heart and life of the church
and the wider community, read *The Micah
Mandate*, by George Grant[48]

Chapter 8

MEDIA:
The Enemy in Our Midst
SILENT NO MORE

> Fifty years ago, British Prime Minister Sir Winston Churchill described an ominous Iron Curtain of communism that had fallen across continental Europe. Today, while that Iron Curtain has lost its former power, another even more destructive force threatens the planet—not with intercontinental ballistic missiles but through ongoing sensory assaults on every human nervous system, heart, and spirit on earth. I call this worldwide blight, the Media Jungle.
>
> —David Chagall

A guest speaker for a youth group at a local church was driving home his point about how powerfully media has shaped our understanding of the world today:

"Who's the character in *Seinfeld* with the funny hair?"

A chorus of hands shot up excitedly. "Kramer!" came the almost universal reply.

"What time does *Friends* come on?"

Again, there was no hesitation. "Eight! Thursday nights. NBC," offered one young lady, nailing the coordinates in both space and time.

"Complete this line from *Spiderman*: 'With great power comes...'"

"Great responsibility!" over seventy-five voices cried in unison.

"Now can someone tell me the difference between rap and hip-hop? Or emo and goth?" There was a brief silence as the audience cast about for the best spokesman to address the nuances of the question. But after a few initial observations were made, the responses again became lively and democratic. Person after person shared either their thoughts on the distinctions or at least illustrated them by identifying their favorite artists in each category.

"OK," the speaker said. "Let's now change gears a bit. Who was the prophet in the Old Testament who had no hair?"

Silence.

"What hour of the day did Jesus die on the cross?" Emboldened by the narrow range of possible answers, a few hands went up and numbers were offered. But it was obvious that nobody really knew.

"Complete this line from Proverbs 3: 'Trust in the Lord with all your heart and...'"

"Obey Him?" the NBC girl offered hopefully.

"Sorry, although obeying Him is certainly a good idea. OK, someone explain to me the difference between justification and sanctification."

The silence among the church's college group was now deafening.

Sound familiar? It should. In fact, such a scene could probably be repeated in *your community*, at *your church*, or maybe even in *your home*. Total media saturation has practically become an American epidemic. It is the cultural air we breathe.

We would have to be Rip van Winkle—just awakened from a decades-long sleep—to not know that a walk down the aisle of a local video store or a quick Google search on the Internet or a few minutes channel-surfing on cable TV is to see that we are in some kind of serious trouble. The words of the poet William B. Yeats—surely no friend of moral clarity himself—are all too sadly being fulfilled before our very eyes:

> We had fed the heart on fantasies,
> The heart's grown brutal from the fare.[1]

Our culture seems to be obsessed and possessed with crass barbarism—with the most blasphemous, relativistic, humanistic, sexually perverse, violent, occultic, and profane forms of entertainment imaginable. As Robert Bork has argued, "Popular entertainment sells sex, pornography, violence, vulgarity, attacks on traditional forms of authority, and outright perversion more copiously and more insistently than ever before in our history. It is no answer to point out that much of popular culture is harmless or even benign. The culture has changed, is changing, and the change is for the worse. The worst is the leading edge."[2]

Remember the recent Super Bowl debacle? Practically a national holiday, pro-football's championship has been called our greatest game, pastime, and ritual—a super-sized and super-charged "public square" where advertisers wait in line to pay $75,000 a second to wave their product before the eyes of 130 million people in the United States and five times that many around the rest of the world. The halftime show at the Super Bowl is always pretty wretched—bad music, bad dancing, very carefully choreographed, colossally expensive immaturity for the lowest common denominator of our Cretan culture.

But the disgusting display in AOL's star-studded lollapalooza in Super Bowl XXXVIII was little more than razzle-dazzle pornography. It was viciously defiling. It was awful. It was brazen, vile, lascivious, craven, offensive, and repugnant—and it completely ruined the rest of the game.

CBS offered a rather meek corporate apology for the "unintentional" nudity in the show. So did the NFL. But that was only the half of it. How about the lyrics? How about the bumping, the grinding, and the S&M outfits? How about the whole disreputable mess? Did they not expect such lowbrow high jinks when they booked the likes of P. Diddy, Nelly, Kid Rock, Janet, and Justin to do the show in the first place?

All apologies aside, MTV, which produced the garish extravaganza, appeared to be completely unrepentant. Before the show even aired, its Web site promised "shocking" moments. And afterward it trumpeted its triumph: "Janet Jackson got nasty." The network's site went on to crow, "Jaws across the country hit the carpet at exactly the same time. You know what we're talking about—Janet Jackson, Justin Timberlake and a kinky finale that rocked the Super Bowl to its core." They even offered "highlight" photos with such captions as, "This pop duo worked harder than the football players!" Now that is something to brag about, isn't it?

So, there we all were. Nearly all of America watched. I watched. My wife and children watched. My students watched. Members of my church watched. Half of the rest of the world watched.

And then there were the ads. Holiday Inn, an all-American hotel chain founded by a Christian, chose as their entry into the sweepstakes of Super Bowl advertising a media spot with a transsexual theme. One of Budweiser's 2004 ads alluded to bestiality. Two other companies hawked drugs touted to help men with "erectile dysfunction."

Even before her infamous "wardrobe malfunction," almost a billion people were assaulted with Janet Jackson singing about a man's "package" (street slang for "sex organ") and how she was "gonna have to ride it tonight." A self-described "bad boy" rapper (with illegitimate children from several different women and a penchant for carrying guns and throwing parties where nude women cavort in the pool) bragged that he was "half man, half drugs. Ask the clubs—bad boy, that's whassup." Another rapper grabbed his crotch while asking his dance partner to "take off all (her) clothes." A self-avowed "pimp" and "trailer-trash" porn connoisseur performed a medley extolling the virtues of "crack heads," "crooked cops," "hookers," and pornography.

Zell Miller, a U.S. senator from Georgia, said this on the floor of the Senate during his Deficit of Decency speech: "Arnold Toynbee, who wrote the acclaimed twelve-volume *A Study of History*, once declared, 'Of the twenty-two civilizations that have appeared in history, nineteen of them collapsed when they reached the moral state America is in today.'"[3] Miller went on to decry the cultural excess which led to "...telecasting around the world made-in-the-USA filth masquerading as entertainment."[4]

Could there be more than a little irony in the fact that all this took place as roughly the same number of people around the world celebrated the most important feast of Islam, *Eid-al-Adha*, the day when Muslims commemorate Abraham's willingness to sacrifice his son? Even as our troops watched the Super Bowl in Iraq—there to defend "truth, justice, and the American way"—we were displaying to the Arab world the ugly side of that "way." Like it or not, large numbers of Muslims see the post-9/11 conflict as a religious war, a struggle between good and evil, Allah and Satan. And there we stood, giving ample evidence that our culture had indeed become demonic.

We certainly have "evolved" from a time when Rhett Butler's use of the word *damn* in *Gone With the Wind* was met with a collective gasp—to a "dumb-and-dumber, numb-and-number" culture where:

- The highest-grossing "family movie" of all time (*E.T. the Extra-Terrestrial*) had an eleven-year-old star who used a grotesque homosexual reference in talking to his brother.

- Two of the most popular teen films of the 1990s went for "laughs" by featuring a character who masturbated into a family dessert (*American Pie*) and one who unwittingly styled her hair with male ejaculate (*There's Something About Mary*).

- The blockbuster *The Silence of the Lambs* managed to make a psychopathic murderer and cannibal one of the surprise "sex symbols" of the year. A decade later, the sequel (*Hannibal*) depicted this same monster sedating a victim and slowly removing and cooking portions of his brain and then feeding it back to him.

And still, that is not the worst of it. Pornography is now a $12 billion business in the United States, larger than the NFL, the NBA, and Major League Baseball combined.[5] There are 4.2 million pornographic Web sites and 372 million pornographic pages generating 68 million daily search engine requests.[6] Now with just a click of a mouse button (often unwittingly), anyone (including children) can have ready access to hard-core sex acts, bestiality, bondage and domination, sadomasochism (including actual torture and mutilation of women for sexual pleasure), scatological acts (defecating and urinating on men or women for sexual pleasure), and child pornography.

So far we have surveyed a whole host of social and cultural problems that are currently plaguing our nation. You may have wondered more than a few times along the way, "How in heaven's name did we get so far down the road to ruin?" I don't think the problem has been so much that "the frog was in the kettle," as that the family was in the living room—glued to the TV. As Lech Walesa has asserted, "History is now shaped by television."[7] We have allowed the enemy into our midst.

A MEDIA PLAY

All too often, statistics bore people. I know. I know. Their eyes just glaze over when you start to tell them about studies or surveys or polls. But like math, statistics are all about magnitude. If you really want to know how big a problem is—or how many resources must be devoted to finding a solution to that problem—you have to be able to measure it somehow. That is what statistics can help us do. The problem of the degradation of our entertainment industry is huge—it is even bigger than we think. So, indulge me for a few minutes here. I've already compiled lots of statistics in this book, and I am about to give you a whole lot more. But, these numbers really are important.

Consider these startling figures: American households with teenage children watch an average of fifty-nine hours of cable and network programming a week. Teens see an average of sixty-seven full-length feature films per year—either in theaters or on video—more than one each week. They own an average of forty-two musical compact discs, sixteen game cartridges, and seven computer games. More than 35 percent of all teens have their own television sets; more than 80 percent own radios; almost 76 percent possess cassette or compact disc players; and while only 39 percent own personal computers, more than 68 percent have access to the Internet.[8] And the numbers are rising rapidly.

This is very serious business. Electronic mass media have become the dominating means of conveying and purveying modern culture among young people. So, what do you think? Is that a good thing? Do you think we should be satisfied with the way this revolution in culture has transpired in our lifetimes?

I have a pretty good hunch that most of us would likely answer with an emphatic "no way." Just to highlight my point, here is another statistic: more than 81 percent of all Americans in a recent poll admitted that they were "seriously concerned" or "uncomfortable" with the direction that modern entertainment has taken of late. Only 2 percent believe that media "should have the greatest influence on children's values."[9] But 67 percent believe that it does—wielding even "greater influence than parents, teachers, coaches, or religious leaders."[10] The pioneering media analyst Marshall McLuhan may not have been very far off the mark when he quipped, "Satan is a great electrical engineer."[11]

According to Neil Postman in *Amusing Ourselves to Death*, a must-read book about modern forms of entertainment, there are two means by which the spirit of a great culture may be undermined—one, portrayed in George Orwell's horrifying novel of oppression, *1984*; the other in Aldous Huxley's equally horrifying novel of debauchery, *Brave New World*.

> In the first—the Orwellian—culture becomes a prison. In the second—the Huxleyan—culture becomes a burlesque....In America, Orwell's prophecies are of small relevance, but Huxley's are well underway toward being realized. For America is engaged in the world's most ambitious experiment to accommodate itself to the technological distractions made possible by the electric plug. This is an experiment that began slowly and modestly in the mid-nineteenth century and has now, in the latter half of the twentieth, reached a perverse maturity in America's consuming love affair with mass media. As nowhere else in the world, Americans have moved far and fast in bringing to a close the age of the slow-moving printed word, and have granted to the media sovereignty over all their institutions. By ushering in the age of television, America has given the world the clearest available glimpse of the Huxleyan future.[12]

It is interesting to me that when God wanted to make His will known to the world, He gave us a book—not a tape series, not a CD, and not a DVD. My wife, Joni, loves to read, and she has taught our children the value of the printed page. Throughout their combined academic careers, they have never received a grade lower than an A. I sincerely believe that their grade averages would be much lower if we had not also taught them the lack of value the media had in their lives.

Postman continued by saying:

> What Orwell feared were those who would ban books. What Huxley feared was that there would be

no reason to ban a book, for there would be no one who wanted to read one. Orwell feared those who would deprive us of information. Huxley feared those who would give us so much that we would be reduced to passivity and egoism. Orwell feared that the truth would be concealed from us. Huxley feared the truth would be drowned in a sea of irrelevance. Orwell feared we would become a captive culture. Huxley feared we would become a trivial culture, preoccupied with feelings instead of facts. As Huxley remarked in *Brave New World Revisited,* the civil libertarians and rationalists who are ever on the alert to oppose tyranny failed to take into account man's almost infinite appetite for distractions. In *1984,* Huxley added, that people are controlled by inflicting pain. In *Brave New World,* they are controlled by inflicting pleasure. In short, Orwell feared that what we hate will ruin us. Huxley feared that what we love will ruin us. We must face the possibility that Huxley, not Orwell, was right.[13]

Indeed, we must. It is not simply a clever slogan; we have actually begun the process of "amusing ourselves to death."[14]

TV, MOVIES, AND MUSIC

Television has become America's drug of choice—a kind of "electronic Valium."[15] And virtually everyone across this vast land is using it. Again, the sheer numbers are worth examining.

More than 98 percent of all households have at least one television set.[16] In fact, more American households have televisions than have indoor plumbing.[17] Not surprisingly, American children watch an inordinate amount of programming. Preschoolers watch an average of more than twenty-seven hours each week—more than four hours per day.[18] On school nights, American teens limit their television consumption to only about three hours per night.[19] In contrast though, they spend about fifty-four minutes on homework, less than sixteen minutes reading, about fourteen minutes alone with their mothers, and less than five minutes with their fathers.[20]

And what is it that we are all watching so obsessively? Sex, dysfunction, perversity, cynicism, skepticism, and anything and everything but moral clarity. There is no use denying it. And then there is the violence: the average American child watches eight thousand made-for-television murders and one hundred thousand acts of violence by the end of grade school.[21] By the time the child has graduated from high school, that number will have doubled.[22] The casual carnage is woven into supposedly real-life situations with amazing alacrity. One survey found that situation comedies, cartoons, and family dramas were just as likely to feature violence as police procedurals, medical dramas, and period masques.[23] As telejournalist David Frost has said, "Television enables you to be entertained in your home by people you wouldn't have in your home."

And this awful barrage is nothing new. While programming has certainly gotten more explicit, more brazen, and more perverse in recent years, television has always been a bastion of mindless barbarism. As early as 1961, Newton N. Minow, at that time the chairman of the Federal Communications Commission, assessed the offering of television in a scathing critique:

> When television is bad, there is nothing worse. I invite you to sit down in front of your television set when your station goes on the air and stay there without a book, magazine, newspaper, profit-and-loss sheet, or rating book to distract you—and keep your eyes glued to that set until the station signs off. I can assure you that you will observe a vast wasteland. You will see a procession of game shows, violence, audience participation shows, formula comedies about totally unbelievable families, blood and thunder, mayhem,

violence, sadism, murder, western badmen, western good men, private eyes, gangsters, more violence, and cartoons. And endlessly, commercials—many screaming, cajoling, and offending. And most of all boredom. True you will see a few things you will enjoy. But they will be very, very few. And if you think I exaggerate, try it.[24]

Eight years later, the Milton Eisenhower Commission reported, "We are deeply troubled by the television's constant portrayal of violence in pandering to a public preoccupation with violence that television itself has helped to generate."[25]

In 1992, the National Commission on Children made a plea for a sane program of internal regulation and self-restraint in the television industry. "Pervasive images of crime, violence, and sexuality expose children and youth to situations and problems that often conflict with the common values of our society. Accordingly, we call upon the media, especially television, to discipline themselves so that they are a part of the solution to our society's serious problems rather than a cause."[26]

Alas, the plea fell on deaf ears. With the proliferation of cable channel options has come a multiplication of the very worst elements of broadcast entertainment from the past—plus, a vastly enlarged menu of offerings heretofore unimagined and unimaginable.

But whatever is wrong with television is doubly wrong with Hollywood films. Television's flimsy restraints on profane language, gratuitous gore, and graphic sexuality are altogether absent in the movies. Things have gone so far that renowned film critic Michael Medved has lamented, "I don't think I can review movies much longer. It is an assault on the senses and an assault on the spirit."[27]

Again, the numbers indicate just how profound the problem really is.

According to a recent nationwide poll, 80 percent of Americans believe that there is too much profanity in Hollywood productions.

More than 60 percent believe there is too much gratuitous violence. About 55 percent believe that graphic sexuality and scatological subjects detract from the value of a film. And 40 percent believe that they have been "desensitized" to issues of moral concern by their viewing habits.[28]

So, why do we watch this stuff? What is the appeal? Amazingly, we continue to patronize the theaters, pay-per-view channels, and video stores in record numbers. Every year there are more than 4 billion videocassette rentals. Almost 2 billion subscribers watched a pay-per-view program last year. And despite rising ticket prices and competition from cable and video rentals, box office receipts have risen every year for the past decade.[29]

And what is it that we are getting for our hard-earned entertainment dollars? Well, the fact is we are consuming more violence, more perversion, and more sacrilege than ever before. According to director Alan Pakula, "Movie violence is like eating salt. The more you eat, the more you need to eat to taste it at all. People are becoming immune to the effects: death counts have quadrupled, the blast power is increasing by the megaton, and they're becoming deaf to it. They've developed an insatiability for raw sensation."[30]

During the early days of Hollywood, the film industry actually regulated itself according to a self-imposed standard of moral restraint designed to uphold social virtue and cultural cohesion. An industry committee, the Hays Association, checked every single film for content expressing "blasphemy, filthy language, explicit eroticism or perversion, superfluous violence or brutality, ethnic slurs, or anti-American sentiment."[31] It made certain that any offensive material was edited out—otherwise, the film was unable to achieve general release to the public. I think it is interesting that a recent liberal so-called *documentary* had anti-American sentiment as its predominant theme, and it met with widespread acclaim—in America.

It is hard for us to imagine this today, but this cooperative association for self-censorship, the Hays Association, sought to uphold community values in virtually every arena that the art of film might touch upon. Hollywood once actually took a voluntary stand for moral clarity! Can you believe it?

According to the Hays Code:

- "The technique of murder must be presented in a way that will not inspire imitation; brutal killings are not to be presented in detail; revenge in modern times shall not be justified."[32]

- "Theft, robbery, safe-cracking, and dynamiting of trains, mines, buildings, etc. should not be detailed in method; arson must be subject to the same safeguards; the use of firearms should be restricted to essentials; methods of smuggling should not be presented."[33]

- "Illegal drug traffic must never be presented."[34]

- "The sanctity of the institution of marriage and the home shall be upheld. Pictures shall not infer that low forms of sex relationship are the accepted or common thing."[35]

- "Adultery, sometimes necessary plot material, must not be explicitly treated or justified, or presented attractively."[36]

- "Scenes of passion should not be introduced when not essential to the plot. In general, passion should be so treated that these scenes do not stimulate the lower and baser element."[37]

- "Seduction or rape should never be more than suggested, and only when essential for the plot, and even then never shown by explicit method; they are never the proper subject for comedy."[38]

- "Sex perversion or inference of it is forbidden."[39]

- "The treatment of low, disgusting, though not necessarily evil subjects, should be subject to the dictates of good taste and regard for the sensibilities of the audience."[40]

- "Obscenity in words, gesture, reference, song, joke, or by suggestion is forbidden."[41]

- "Pointed vulgarity or vulgar expressions, however used, are forbidden."[42]

- "Complete nudity is never permitted. This includes nudity in fact, or in silhouette, or any lecherous or licentious notice thereof by other characters in the picture."[43]

- "No film or episode may throw ridicule on any religious faith."[44]

- "Ministers of religion, in their character as such, should not be used as comic characters or as villains."[45]

Critics might try to argue that under such stringent guidelines, no great films could ever be made. I can almost hear the Hollywood moguls moaning and groaning in disbelief now.

The fact is though, all of Hollywood's greatest classics were made according to the standards of the Hays Code: *All Quiet on the Western Front, It's a Wonderful Life, The Good Earth, Stagecoach, Sergeant York, The Grapes of Wrath, Mr. Smith Goes to Washington, It Happened One Night, Mutiny on the Bounty, Moby Dick, Gone With the Wind, Citizen Kane, Watch on the Rhine, The Thirty-Nine Steps, For Whom the Bell Tolls, Casablanca, A Tree Grows in Brooklyn, Miracle on 34th Street, Key Largo, All the King's Men, The African Queen, The*

Maltese Falcon, A Place in the Sun, An American in Paris, High Noon, On the Waterfront, East of Eden, Stalag 17, and *From Here to Eternity.* During the entire span of Hollywood's "Golden Age" the Hays Code was honored.

But no more. It seems that Hollywood filmmakers go out of their way to see how far they can stretch the viewing public's tolerance for taboo. In the films of yesteryear, actors and actresses actually had to practice their craft instead of participating in sex, violence, more sex, and more violence. Indeed, one heralded, Oscar-winning screenwriter and director asserted, "I prefer rude, rowdy stuff because that's one of the easiest ways to conquer an audience's disbelief. The more realistic the violence and the steamier the sex, the more likely you will be to forget you are watching a film."[46]

No wonder the Hollywood establishment worked double overtime to try to trash Mel Gibson's *The Passion of the Christ.*

But if there is anything that may actually have more influence over our culture than TV and movies, it is music. Music captures the heart. It is a powerful, spiritual force. It can be a tool of great good or a weapon of great destruction. The great Scottish literary historian Thomas Carlyle once said, "Sing me the songs of a generation, and I'll tell you the soul of the times."[47]

Part of the problem with Carlyle's proposition is that too much of our popular music is not actually even singable. Not only is it often without recognizable tune, pitch, cadence, or tenor—and even without melody, harmony, or regular rhythm—but it is also so profane that it is unrepeatable. Many rap and rock songs have gone far beyond the mere bounds of pornography to vile brutality, scatological filth, sadistic nihilism, blasphemous irreverence, and provocative decadence.

Pop music has almost always been sentimental, sappy, and insubstantial. In the forties it tended to be romantic. In the fifties it was silly. In the sixties it was psychedelic. In the seventies it was carnal. In the eighties it was sensual. In the nineties it was chaotic. Now, it has become nightmarishly barbaric. With the advent of grunge rock, hip-hop, goth rock, gangsta rap, death metal, and speed metal, a new wave of wildly angry music—with minimal melody lines or hooks, harsh and distorted electronics, incessant syncopations, and vile lyrics—has swept on to center stage.

Steeped in a hopeless worldview of suicide, occultism, sexual abuse, self-mutilation, brutal sadism, and random revenge, the music is depressing, dark, and deleterious. High-volume, deliberately disgusting, and offensive "shock jocks" profile the music and its irreverent lifestyle, its devil-may-care worldview, and its slovenly fashion sense in music videos and over FM radio stations.

This is what our nation's kids are listening to; this is what they are downloading from iTunes; this is what they are swapping on the Internet; and this is what they have on their iPods. No wonder the song of the soul of America is so dissonant.

According to Michael Bywater, "The music industry has somehow reduced humanity's greatest achievement—a near universal language of pure transcendence—into a knuckle-dragging sub-pidgin of grunts and snarls, capable of fully expressing only the more pointless forms of violence and the more brutal forms of sex."[48]

A steady diet of that kind of music is likely to have a terrible effect on anyone—but it especially impacts impressionable adolescents. And teens have more than a steady diet of it: between the seventh and twelfth grades, the average American teen listens to 10,500 hours of rock music, just slightly less than the total number of hours spent in the classroom from kindergarten to graduation.[49]

According to the Council on Scientific Affairs of the American Medical Association, "Over the past decade the messages portrayed by certain types of rock music may well present a real threat to the physical health and well-being of especially vulnerable children and adolescents. Lyrics promoting drug and alcohol abuse, sexual exploitation, bigotry, and racism are combined with rhythms and intensities that appeal to youth. Physicians should know about these potentially destructive themes."[50]

Indeed, we should all know about them.

CONDITIONING PROCESS

Add to television, movies, and music the violent or perverse content
in many video games and Internet sites, and you have a prescription
for cultural disaster. At every turn the vision, the standards, and the
precepts that provoked the great flowering of Western civilization are
subverted—and that makes for a terribly unstable society.

In essence what we have done is brainwash our children to hate
our culture, to hate our mores, to hate beauty and significance, to
hate authority and substance, to hate us, and to hate each other.

Syndicated journalist Charles Krauthammer has said it well:

> Today's mass culture would not know an idea, sub-
> versive or otherwise, if it met one. It traffics instead
> in sensibility and image, with a premium on the
> degrading: rap lyrics in which women are for us-
> ing and abusing, movies in which violence is ad-
> ministered with a smirk and a smile. Casual cruelty,
> knowing sex. Nothing could be better designed to
> rob youth of its most ephemeral gift: innocence.
> The ultimate effect of our mass culture is to make
> children older than their years, to turn them into
> the knowing, cynical pseudo-adult that is by now
> the model kid of the TV sitcom. It is a crime against
> children to make them older than their years. And
> it won't do for the purveyors of cynicism to hide
> behind the First Amendment. Of course they have
> the right to publish and peddle this trash to kids.
> But they should have the decency not to.[51]

AN EPIDEMIC OF CONTEMPT

Perhaps that is why our society has become such an inhospitable place.
Once upon a time, American culture was actually recognized far and
wide for its genial hospitality, gracious sincerity, and friendly warmth.

While always gregarious, ardent, and demonstrative, that enthusiasm invariably seemed to be tempered with a contagious sociability.

Abraham Kuyper, the remarkable Dutch pastor who became a journalist and then an educator and statesman, visited the United States just before he became prime minister of the Netherlands at the turn of the century. He was struck by the fact that, "The average American is by no means hidebound by the formal conventions of European pomp and protocol, which can, after all, prove to be rather stuffy at times. Nevertheless, he is affable, cordial, and companionable. His good nature is pleasantly evident and his honest character is genially transparent."[52]

Likewise, John Buchan, the Scottish diplomat and literary genius, visited America in the service of King George just prior to the Second World War. He observed that, "The common courtesy of Americans is everywhere obvious. In the shops and upon the streets, at work and at play, in the midst of their hurly-burly and their hustle-bustle, they are invariably considerate, polite, respectful, and mannerly."[53]

But it appears that those days are all but gone. Observers of the contemporary American scene are often struck by the grating incivility of our conduct. More often than not we are rude and crude to one another, mocking and disrespectful to due authority, and irreverent and baleful to time-honored convention. We often appear to be hasty and unconcerned about practically anything and everything but our own agendas.

As the English journalist Thomas Garton has remarked, "The qualities that have made America so attractive, so vibrant, and so dynamic to the rest of the world are the very qualities that seem to be undermined by the current wave of grunge pop culture. The maleficent, brash, and punkish air of the rabble has made its way into the mainstream of American life. Children are hardly ever taught manners these days. There is nary a 'Yes, Sir. No, Sir.' or a 'Thank you very much.' to be found. Even the mild-mannered suburbanite seems to fly into a rage on the interstate when another driver somehow impedes his progress. Race divides acrimoniously. The 'suits' are pitted against the 'workers.' And the everyday conversations of ordinary folks are laced with unnoticed obscenity."[54]

While most of us still make every effort to be decent, hardworking, and upstanding citizens, the effects of this ever-widening culture of impertinence are felt by us all. There is practically no escaping them. They are all too obvious in our business affairs, our community interactions, and our interpersonal relationships.

Ultimately, they contribute to a divisive, dehumanizing, and disrespectful social environment—one that may even stoke the flames of disaffection and violence among our children. "Why should a child respect the feelings, the dignity, or even the life of another child," asks Bethel College sociologist Adeline Lang, "if respect has ceased to be an important component part of a culture's civil or social vocabulary?"[55]

Indeed, she asserts, "By failing to impress on young people the value of politeness, consideration, and courtesy we are actually inadvertently reinforcing patterns of incivility, animosity, and strife. The pop psychology emphasis of the past two decades or so on self-fulfillment, self-actualization, self-realization, and self-expression has created a barbarous atmosphere where, at least subconsciously, most people are much more concerned about themselves, their interests, and their concerns than they are about those of others. That makes for a volatile situation—especially among the young."[56]

THE FIFTH COLUMN

In 1936, Spain was ravaged by a great civil war. Emilio Mola, one of the leaders of the Nationalist Army under the command of Francisco Franco, surrounded the capital city of Madrid with columns to the north, south, east, and west. When asked from which direction he expected the city to be taken, Mola replied, *"Una quinta columna."*[57] This "fifth column" was made up of the spies and propaganda he had managed to plant within the city of Madrid itself.

It is all too evident that there is a civil war going on for the destiny of our nation, our culture, and our civilization—one that this generation will lose if the "fifth column" of popular perversity continues to flourish in our hearts, our homes, and our lives.

The great Russian novelist Fyodor Dostoyevsky observed that when untethered from the Christian worldview, art would begin by imitating life. But then life would start to imitate art and then would finally draw the very reason for its existence from the arts.[58] Historian Daniel Boorstin sounded a similar alarm when he warned that Americans increasingly live in a world where fantasy is more real than reality. "We risk," he said, "being the first people in history to have been able to make their illusions so vivid, so persuasive, so 'realistic' that they can live in them."[59]

Perhaps we really are "amusing ourselves to death." Perhaps we really have invited the enemy into our midst.

ACTION POINTS

- Visit www.mediawatch.com to learn about more about this issue.

- Review media ratings to make educated decisions for yourself and your family.

- Visit www.pluggedinonline.com for good reviews on movies, television, and music.

- *World Magazine Online* has a section entitled "culture beat," which is a good source for movie and television reviews. Visit their Web site at www.worldmag.com.

- Visit www.kids-in-mind.com for movie reviews for the entire family.

- Write letters to local media outlets objecting to obvious bias against morality.

- Contact the FCC to file indecency complaints against media outlets at www.fcc.gov.

- Recommended reading:
  Hollywood vs. America, by Michael Medved[60]

Not Just a Dream, but a Vision

SILENT NO MORE

It was T. E. Lawrence, the man better known as Lawrence of Arabia, who once said, "All men dream: but not equally. Those who dream by night in the dusty recesses of their minds wake in the day to find that it was vanity: but the dreamers of the day are dangerous men, for they may act their dream with open eyes, to make that possible. This I did."[1]

I have known many dreamers in my life, but most of them were the kind that T. E. Lawrence described. They dreamed, but they did not act their dream. Their dreams remained little more than imaginings because they were not pulled to earth and made flesh and blood by action.

I have known some men who dreamed but made their dreams reality. These men had a dream, but they also had a vision, a plan of action. Their dreams changed the world because they knew how to wed dream to action through the power of a vision.

This is what I seek to do. I dream of an America built upon the foundation our fathers established, but not limited to it. I dream of a land where faith is vibrant, where wise men rule, where moral boundaries are preserved, where our schools build champions, where our economy thrives, where men of all races achieve, and where we are the example to the world we are called to be.

This is what I dream, but I know that it will not be so by dreaming alone. We must act. And we must act wisely. In fact, I must tell you that I fear that some will read this book and act foolishly, more than I fear that they will not read this book at all. I have seen over the years the damage done by foolish people and their unwise actions, even in the service of a wise cause. And I know what harm it does, what ridicule it deserves, and what destruction it brings.

The last thing I want to be is another screaming voice moving people to extremes and provoking them to folly in the name of patriotism. I am trying to move people, first, to compassion, then to wisdom, and then to duty. Without all three—compassion, wisdom, and duty—our country has no hope.

I know that some will be surprised at my call for compassion, for they tend to see people of my views as harsh and cold-hearted. Nothing could be further from the truth.

In fact, let me take a risk here as I close this book. I want to share a story from my family life, one that will illustrate not only what I have been through, but that also may explain why I approach the matters of our national life—the ones I have addressed in this book—with such concern for the suffering of individuals.

In 1997, my wife and I lost a child. Her name was Abigail, and her loss is a stab to the heart that we feel even to this day. I would like to let my wife's words tell the tale, though. I believe she, far better than I, will be able to capture the pain, the disappointment, and the desperate clinging to hope. My wife's name is Joni, and she is an amazing lady. She's the mother of my children, and she's the greatest Christian that I know. She exemplifies the life and heart of Jesus Christ. With grace in every gesture and heaven in her eyes, she has been more than the "little lady" behind the visible man. She has been my partner, my mentor, and my dearest earthly love. Here are her words:

There is nothing in life, I feel, that changes the fabric of your existence quite like tragedy. While it may not define you, surviving tragedy will forever mark you. The wounds may heal, but the scars remain as a reminder of God's grace and strength that led you through "the valley of the shadow of death."

There is a vast and indescribable difference between an unwanted pregnancy and the unwanted loss of one. When my husband and I suffered a miscarriage in 1997, I discovered a bewildering irony in the church. The very same Christians who waved their prolife banners and wore their buttons and bumper stickers with militant pride were the very same ones who dismissed the loss of my "wanted" pregnancy as though I had the common cold.

The devastation that I felt over the loss of this little life was suffocating—every breath seemed a conscious effort. My once tranquil soul became a tidal wave of emotion as grief washed over every ounce of my being. This was not just the loss of a pregnancy; this was the loss of my baby, my child, my teenager, my married daughter, and the mother of my grandchildren. A loss of life, yes, but a loss of a life, *and a lifetime even more so,* became the anthem of my heart's cry.

I woke up each day wishing I hadn't. I knew, though, that my other two children needed me. I pushed the *autopilot* button and went through the proverbial motions of our daily routine. Where many others were concerned, I was met with sympathy, but I mostly recall their sometimes unfeeling remarks: "Well, at least you never knew the baby." "At least you never bonded." "You'll be together in heaven." "You can try again soon and have another baby."

If I had been rude, I guess I could have responded, "Yes, I knew my baby and fell in love with her the moment I knew she was *alive* on the inside of me." "Yes, we bonded; I talked to her all day. I told her stories about her brother and sister and how I throw the grandest of birthday parties and how fun Christmas is at our house. I told her how great her daddy is and that she would totally wrap him around her finger and get everything she wanted like her brother and sister do. I told her about her wonderful family and how excited we would be to see her. I told her about Jesus and that I was sure she was one of His angels that He was sending to me. And yes, I thank God for the blessed assurance that I will hold her in heaven, but I want to hold her here on earth, and if that's selfish, so be it." "And no, I can't try again for another baby, and even if I could, this is the one I want."

All I wanted was my baby and for someone to understand and to validate the life and loss. This life was precious, and the loss so painful and unique. There is no funeral, no memorial, no closure, yet such emptiness; nowhere or no way was provided to announce to the world, "This is our child, and she is no longer with us."

She wasn't just fetal tissue; she was alive. I saw her heart beating in an ultrasound one day and not beating in an ultrasound another day. I looked at her lifeless body on the screen and said my goodbyes. That is all I had, a life one day and a death another. I promised our baby that her life would be a ministry and that Mommy would always help others who lost their little angels, too. We honor her life and her memory. People cope in different ways. I have always coped through purpose, finding a way to serve through my pain to others in need.

My perspective as well as my priorities are so different. I "don't sweat the small stuff." Each day is a gift, and when much has been taken from you, you appreciate everything that you are given.

God is the God of amazing grace, and through that valley I learned and I grew, but I never forgot. We planted a weeping willow tree in our baby's honor, and every year we sponsor a student in our preparatory school who would have been our child's classmate. No one has ever known—it has been my private memorial in hopes of honoring her and giving her life purpose. I know she would have wanted it that way.

I share these tender words with you to make this point. Those of us who call for the ancient boundaries to be observed in this generation, who wish to hold on to holy ways and wise governance—we are not immune to suffering ourselves. And sometimes, it is just this personal suffering that makes us yearn for a society that is not increasing the suffering of millions.

I stand against poverty because I know its sting, and I yearn for people to be free from it. I stand against abortion because I have lost a child, and I grieve that more than four thousand other children are lost intentionally through abortion every day in America. I stand against sexual perversion and those who spread it, because I know the devastation it brings to human souls. I call for what is now called *a conservative view of public policy* because it protects people from the control and impoverishment of a socialist society. And I stand against the folly of the Church because I know that the greatness of the Church may still arise if the folly is named for what it is. I love the Church. I am a churchman in the broadest sense. But I also know it was a failure of the Church and her people that deepened my wife's hurt when we lost our child. I want better: for our nation, for the Church, and for the suffering hearts of the world.

Martin Niemoeller, a Lutheran pastor in Germany prior to World War II, commented on the days leading up to that terrible conflict:

> In Germany, the Nazis first came for the Communists, and I didn't speak up because I wasn't a Communist. Then they came for the Jews, and I didn't speak up because I wasn't Jewish. Then they came for the trade unionists, and I didn't speak up because I wasn't a trade unionist. Then they came for the Catholics, and I didn't speak up because I was a Protestant. Finally, they came for me, but there was no one left to speak up.[2]

Adolph Hitler became angered by Neimoeller's rebellious sermons and had him arrested in 1937. Neimoeller was tried the following year and then sentenced to seven months in prison. Then Hitler ordered him arrested again, and Neimoeller spent the next seven years in concentration camps.[3] If you think something like that can't happen in America, think again. If you live with perversion long enough, it begins to seem normal and right—even if it is abnormal and wrong.

So I have chosen to be silent no more. It is my hope that you will do the same. Speak for those who cannot speak. Speak from your pain what others cannot know. Speak the wisdom of the ancients in a world enamored of the new. And speak the truth of God to those who know only the answers of this secular age. Remember, if we are silent much longer, we may not be able to speak out at all.

Join me. Be silent no more. Our times demand it. Our history compels it. Our future requires it. And God is watching.

NOTES

PROLOGUE:
It's Showtime

1. CNN.com Election 2004, http://www.cnn.com/ELECTION/2004/pages/results/states/US/P/00/epolls.0.html (accessed December 3, 2004).

2. CNN.com Election 2004, Ballot Measures, http://www.cnn.com/ELECTION/2004/pages/results/ballot.measures/ (accessed December 3, 2004).

3. CNN.com Election 2004, U.S. President/Oregon, http://www.cnn.com/ELECTION/2004/pages/results/states/OR/P/00/index.html (accessed December 3, 2004).

4. Political Humor—Jokes, Satire, and Political Cartoons, http://politicalhumor.about.com/library/graphics/jesusland.jpg (accessed December 3, 2004).

5. CNN.com Election 2004, Ballot Measures, http://www.cnn.com/ELECTION/2004/pages/results/ballot.measures/ (accessed December 3, 2004).

6. Ibid.

7. Ibid.

INTRODUCTION:
The Commitment of Our Fathers, the Calling of Our Times

1. Office of the Press Secretary, The White House, "President's Remarks at National Day of Prayer and Remembrance," National Cathedral, Washington, DC, September 14, 2001, http://www.whitehouse.gov/news/releases/2001/09/20010914-2.html.

CHAPTER 1: JUDICIAL TYRANNY
The Genius of Our Fathers, the Folly of Our Times

1. Nancy Gibbs, "The Faith Factor," *Time*, June 21, 2004.

2. Henry Steele Commager, ed., *Documents of American History* (New York: Appleton-Century-Crofts, Inc., 1949).

3. Benjamin Franklin speech at the Constitutional Convention, June 28, 1787. At http://www.geocities.com/peterroberts.geo/Relig-Politics/BFranklin.html#quo.

4. Rus Walton, *Biblical Principles* (Plymouth, MA: Plymouth Rock Foundation, 1984), 357.

5. Congress, Senate, Joint Committee on Printing, *Washington's Farewell Address to the People of the United States*, prepared by the Legislative Reference Service, 96th Congress, 1st session, 1979, Senate Document No. 5.

6. Quoted in John Eidsmoe, *Christianity and the Constitution* (Grand Rapids, MI: Baker Book House, 1987), 273.

7. Robert Cord, *Separation of Church and State: Historical Fact and Current Fiction* (New York: Lambeth Press, 1982), 6.

8. Jonathan Elliott, *Debates on the Federal Constitution* (Philadelphia: J. B. Lippincott, Co., 1901), 2:553.

9. Ibid., 3:659.

10. Ibid., 1:328.

11. Ibid., 1:334; 4:244.

12. *Annals of the Congress of the United States: The Debates and Proceedings in the Congress of the United States*, compiled from authentic materials by Joseph Gales, Senior (Washington, DC: Gales and Seaton, 1834), 1:434; hereafter referred to as *Annals of the Congress*.

13. Michael J. Malbin, *Religion and Politics: The Intentions of the Authors of the First Amendment* (Washington, DC: American Enterprise Institute for Public Policy Research, 1978), 12.

14. Ibid., 12–13.

15. Malbin, *Religion and Politics*, 12.

16. Quoted in John Eidsmoe, *The Christian Legal Advisor* (Milford, MI: Mott Media, 1984), 133–164.

17. Ibid.

18. Ibid., 121.

19. General Assembly of the Presbyterian Church in the USA, May 26, 1789. Transcript at Mount Vernon Archives.

20. Alfred Meyer, "The Blaine Amendment and the Bill of Rights," *Harvard Law Review 64* (1951): 944–945.

21. *Everson v. Board of Education*, 330 U.S. 1 (1947).

22. Ibid.

23. Ibid.

24. Partial-Birth Abortion Act of 2003 (enrolled as agreed to or passed by both House and Senate) at the first session of the One Hundred Eighth Congress of the United States of America on Tuesday, the seventh day of January, two thousand and three. See http://www.nrlc.org/abortion/pba/partial_birth_abortion_Ban_act_final_language.htm.

25. Judge Phyllis Hamilton's opinion declaring the Partial-Birth Abortion Ban unconstitutional, in *Human Events Online*, the National Conservative weekly. See http://www.humaneventsonline.com/article.php?id=4128.

26. Author's paraphrase of Judge Phyllis Hamilton's opinion declaring the Partial-Birth Abortion Ban unconstitutional.

27. See U.S. Supreme Court, *ex parte McCardle*, 74 U.S. 506 (Wall.) (1868) at http://www.constitution.org/ussc/074-506.htm.

28. Pat Robertson, *Courting Disaster: How the Supreme Court is Usurping the Power of Congress and the People* (Nashville, TN: Integrity Publishers, 2004).

CHAPTER 2: RACE
Fulfilling Our Fathers' Dream

1. From the National Vital Statistics Report, Vol. 52, No. 10, December 17, 2003, at http://www.cdc.gov/nchs/data/nvsr/nvsr52/nvsr52_10t12.pdf.

2. See Deuteronomy 7:6 and Isaiah 66:18–19.

3. Read Obadiah 10–16.

4. Curtis Lawrence, "Race Pay Gap Persists at All Grad Levels," *Chicago Sun-Times*, January 4, 2004.

5. Lerone Bennett, *Before the Mayflower: a History of Black America* (New York: Penguin, 1984).

6. Stephen Mansfield, *Then Darkness Fled: The Liberating Wisdom of Booker T. Washington* (Nashville, TN: Cumberland House Publishing, 1999).

CHAPTER 3: POVERTY
The American Century: A Golden Age?

1. *Forbes*, September 14, 1992; *WorldNet Daily*, May 24, 2004.

2. Henry R. Luce, "The American Century," *Life*, February 17, 1941.

3. David S. Broder, "Bush Accepts Nomination, Vows to Fulfill Reagan 'Mission'; Candidate Pledges To Create Jobs, Work for Peace," Washington Post, August 19, 1988.

4. Dan Balz, "'No One...Doubts Us Anymore' Bush Tells Gulf Vets," *Washington Post*, March 18, 1991.

5. Paul Johnson, "An Awakened Conscience," *Forbes*, September 14, 1992.

6. Lenore J. Weitzman, *The Divorce Revolution: The Unexpected Social and Economic Consequences for Women and Children in America*, 2nd ed. (New York: The Free Press, 1999), ix.

7. Ibid., xii.

8. Community Service Society of New York Bulletin, April 2002.

9. Ibid.

10. Stop News, American Life League, July 2003.

11. Ibid.

12. Harold Frelton and Gerry Yarborough, eds., *The Crisis in American Health Care*, (New York: U.S. Resources, 1993), 3.

13. Ibid.

14. Ibid.

15. Ibid.

16. Ibid.

17. Ibid., 4.

18. Ibid.

19. Ibid.

20. Lyndon Baines Johnson, "State of the Union 1964," From Revolution to Reconstruction...and what happened afterwards, http:// odur.let.rug.nl/~usa/P/lj36/speeches/su64lbj.htm

21. Karen Hawthorne, *The Alms Race* (New York: Garden Valley, 1968), 62.

22. Charles Murray, *Losing Ground*, (New York: Basic Books, 1985), 24–40.

23. Ibid., 8.

24. Ibid.

25. *Welfare Reform Journal*, April 1991.

26. Ibid.

27. Ibid.

28. Stuart Butler and Anna Kondratas, *Out of the Poverty Trap* (New York: Free Press, 1987), 1–27.

29. *Welfare Reform Journal*, April 1991.

30. Ibid.

31. Murray, *Losing Ground*, 3–9.

32. George Grant, *Bringing in the Sheaves* (Brentwood, TN: Wolgemuth and Hyatt, 1989).

33. George Grant, *The Dispossessed: Homelessness in America* (Wheaton, IL: Crossway, 1986).

34. Marvin Olasky, *The Tragedy of American Compassion* (Wheaton, IL: Crossway, 1992).

35. George Gilder, *Wealth and Poverty* (New York: Basic, 1991).

36. *Welfare Reform Journal*, April 1991.

37. Ibid.

38. Ibid.

39. Ibid.

40. Thomas Sowell, *Civil Rights* (New York: Morrow, 1984).

41. Walter Williams, *The State Against the Blacks* (New York: McGraw, 1982).

42. Barry Bluestone and Bennett Harrison, *The Deindustrialization of America* (New York: Basic, 1982).

43. Author interview, October 19, 1998.

44. *Wall Street Journal*, November 12, 1982.

45. Ibid.

46. Ibid.

47. Author interview, October 19, 1998.

48. Ibid.

49. Marian Wright Edelman, *Families in Peril: An Agenda for Social Change* (Cambridge, MA: Harvard University, 1987), 71.

50. Murray, *Losing Ground*.

51. *Welfare Reform Journal*, April 1991.

52. Ibid.

53. Ibid.

54. Author interview, October 19, 1998.

55. Grant, *Dispossessed*, 165–186.

56. Grant, *Bringing in the Sheaves*, 53–79.

57. Vernon Carter, *The New Deal and Beyond* (New York: Lathrop and Harrod, 1979), 169.

58. Henry Cabot Lodge, *Alexander Hamilton* (New York: Charles Scribner's and Sons, 1898), 57.

59. Ibid.

60. Ibid., 62.

61. Michael Harrington, *The New American Poverty* (New York: Holt, Rinehart, and Winston, 1984).

62. Jonathan Kozol, *Rachel and Her Children* (New York: Crown, 1988).

63. Ibid.

64. Murray Rothbard, *For a New Liberty* (New York: Macmillan, 1973), 86.

65. Ibid.

66. Ibid.

67. The responsibility for Christians to care for the poor is stressed throughout the Scriptures:

Exodus 22:25	Leviticus 19:10	Leviticus 23:22
Leviticus 25:35–37	Numbers 18:24	Numbers 24:14
Deuteronomy 14:29	Deuteronomy 15:1–2	Deuteronomy 24:19–21
Ruth 2:1–23	Ruth 4:1–12	Psalm 41:1–3
Proverbs 11:25	Proverbs 14:21	Proverbs 14:31
Proverbs 17:5	Proverbs 21:13	Proverbs 22:9
Proverbs 28:27	Proverbs 29:7	Proverbs 31:8–9
Isaiah 1:10–17	Isaiah 10:1–2	Isaiah 32:6–8
Isaiah 58:1–12	Amos 5:1–27	Matthew 5:16
Matthew 7:12	Matthew 10:8	Matthew 25:31–46
Mark 12:44	Luke 3:11	Luke 6:38
Luke 9:48	Luke 10:30–37	Luke 11:41
Luke 12:33–34	Acts 20:35	Romans 12:8–20
2 Corinthians 1:3–4	2 Corinthians 8:1–24	2 Corinthians 9:7
Galatians 5:6	Galatians 6:2	Galatians 6:9–10
Ephesians 5:2	Ephesians 2:8–10	2 Thessalonians 3:6–10
1 Timothy 5:8	1 Timothy 6:18–19	Titus 2:11–14
Titus 3:1	Titus 3:8	Titus 3:14
Hebrews 13:16	James 2:14–26	1 John 3:17

68. Charles Haddon Spurgeon, *John Plowman's Pictures* (Philadelphia: John Altemus, n.d.), 165.

69. *National Reform Association Newsgram*, December 1993.

CHAPTER 4: HOMOSEXUALITY
The Unhappy Gay Agenda

1. "Gay Marriage? George Grant Focuses on Solutions to Homosexuality," *Declaration Foundation: Restoring America*, January 26, 2004, http://www.declaration.net/news.asp?docID=3977.

2. Ibid.

3. Ibid.

4. Ibid.

5. Ibid.

6. Ibid.

7. J. P. Paul, et al., *American Journal of Public Health* 92(8) (August 2002): 1338–1345.

8. P. Cameron, K. Cameron, and K. Proctor, *Psychological Report* 64(3 Pt 2), PMID #2765461 (June 1989): 1167–1179.

9. K. E. Ernulf and S. M. Innala, *Arch Sexual Behavior* 24(6), PMID #8572912 (December 1995): 631–654.

10. *American Spectator*, August 1984.

11. George Grant and Mark Horne, *Legislating Immorality: The Homosexual Movement Comes Out of the Closet* (Chicago: Moody Press, 1993), 109–141.

12. Ibid.

13. Franklin Payne, *What Every Christian Should Know About the AIDS Epidemic: The Medical and Biblical Facts* (Augusta, GA: Covenant, 1991), 71–72.

14. Ibid.

15. Ibid.

16. Ibid.

17. Tony Marco, *Gay Rights: A Public Health Disaster and Civil Wrong* (Ft. Lauderdale, FL: Coral Ridge, 1992), 13.

18. Ibid., 14.

19. Excerpts from *Time*, August 3, 1992, quoted in Julianne Hamden, "Mycoplasma Fermentans (Incognitus) and AIDS, Chronic Fatigue Syndrome, and Gulf War Syndrome—More Questions Remain," Possible Anthrax Vaccine Dangers Information, http://www.nccn.net/~wwithin/anthrax.htm.

20. L. McKusick, W. Horstman, and T. J. Coates, "AIDS and Sexual Behavior Reported by Gay Men in San Francisco," *American Journal of Public Health* 75 (December 1985): 493–496.

21. Malcolm Gladwell, "Failures Seen in Education on 'Safe Sex'; AIDS Experts Worry as Warnings Ignored," *Washington Post*, June 24, 1990.

22. Frank Browning, *The Culture of Desire: Paradox and Perversity in Gay Lives Today* (New York: Crown, 1993), 119.

23. R. S. Hogg, et al., *Modelling the Impact of HIV Disease on Mortality in Gay and Bisexual Men*, British Columbia Centre for Excellence in HIV/AIDS, St Paul's Hospital, Vancouver, Canada.

24. Ibid.

25. *Family Research Newsletter*, April–June 1991.

26. Ibid.

27. Ibid.

28. Ibid.

29. Ibid.

30. Ibid.

31. Hogg, op. cit.

32. Judith Reisman, *Kinsey, Sex, and Fraud* (Lafayette, LA: Huntington House, 1990).

33. Hara Estroff Marano, "Sexual Issues Fan Parents' Fears," *New York Times*, July 2, 1997.

34. D. J. McKirnan and P. L. Peterson, *Addictive Behaviour* 14(5), PMID #2589133 (1989): 545–553.

35. *National Christian Times*, March 2004.

36. Dr. David Innis, *CFV Report*, Vol. 10, November 1993.

37. Steve Warren, "Warning to the Homophobes," *The Advocate*, September 1987, as quoted in "Sodomy—the Pride of Liberal Secularism," GAIDS Shema Israel, http://sami119.tripod.com/shemaisrael/id23.html.

38. Ibid.

39. Ibid.

40. *The Tennessean*, October 11, 1993.

41. Rachel Schwing, *Hate Crimes Statistics*, New York Family Research Foundation, nyfrf.org, 1997.

42. *Washington Action Alert*, November 1993.

43. Ibid.

44. David Limbaugh, *Persecution: How Liberals Are Waging War Against Christianity* (Washington, DC: Regnery Publishing, 2003).

45. Ibid.

46. Ibid.

47. *World*, March 6, 1993

48. Ibid.

49. *Time*, August 17, 1992.

50. *World*, March 6, 1993.

51. *Human Events*, December 18, 1993, as quoted in Tony Marco, "Recent Media Reaction, Gay and Straight, Supports the Arguments Made in This Analysis," *Special Class Protections for Self-Alleged Gays: A Question of "Orientation" and Consequences*, Leadership University, http://www .leaderu.com/marco/special/spc57.html.

52. Ibid.

53. Ibid.

54. Ibid.

55. Ibid.

56. *Washington Blade*, March 12, 1993.

57. *New Yorker*, November 9, 1992.

58. *World Net Daily*, June 17, 2004.

59. Susan Jones, "Mrs. Kerry Would Focus on 'Gay Tolerance' as First Lady," Cybercast News Service, CNSNews.com, October 19, 2004, http://www.cnsnews.com/Culture/archive/200410/CUL20041019b.html (accessed December 6, 2004).

60. Andrew Sullivan, *New Republic*, quoted in Steven Menashi, "Matters of Life and Death," *The Dartmouth Review*, editorial, March 12, 2001, http://www.theamericanscene.com/pubs/tdr31201.html. Also, Phil Brennan, "Media Push Homosexuality as Part of P.C. Agenda," NewsMax .com, http://www.newsmax.com/archives/articles/2002/2/8/165348.shtml.

61. *New Yorker*, November 9, 1992.

62. Ibid.

63. *Tennessean*, October 11, 1993.

64. Ibid.

65. *Christian News-Observer*, Spring 1988.

66. George Grant, *The 57% Solution* (Franklin, TN: Adroit Press, 1993), 90–110.

67. R. Albert Mohler Jr., "Criminalizing Christianity: Sweden's Hate Speech Law," Alex Jones' Prison Planet.com, August 6, 2004, http://www .prisonplanet.com/articles/august2004/060804criminalizingchristianity .htm.

68. Peter Sprigg and Timothy Dailey, eds., *Getting It Straight* (Washington DC: Family Research Council, 2004).

CHAPTER 5: ISLAM
The Deception of Allah

1. George Grant, *The Last Crusader: The Untold Story of Christopher Columbus* (Wheaton, IL: Crossway Books, 1992), 66.

2. Jonathan Edwards, *The Works of Jonathan Edwards* (Edinburgh: The Banner of Truth Trust, 1979), 607.

3. A. B. C. Whipple, *To the Shores of Tripoli* (Annapolis, MD: Naval Institute Press, 1991), 38.

4. Genesis 27:40; 16:12, NIV

5. Reuven Paz, *The Project for the Research for Islamist Movements (PRISM)*, Vol. 2, No. 3, October 19, 2004.

6. Ibid.

7. Ibid.

8. The historical information about the beginning of Islam is adapted from Karen Armstrong, *Islam* (New York: Modern Library, 2000).

9. Ibid.

10. Martin Lings, *Muhammad, His Life Based on the Earliest Sources* (Rochester, Vermont: Inner Traditions International, 1983), 43.

11. *The Quran*, Surah 96:1–5.

12. Lings, *Muhammad*.

13. Huston Smith, *The World's Religions* (San Francisco: Harper, 1991), 226.

14. Karen Armstrong, *Muhammad: A Biography of the Prophet* (San Francisco: Harper, 1992), 85.

15. Lings, *Muhammad,* 44.

16. George Grant, *The Blood of the Moon* (Nashville, TN: Nelson Books, 2001), 46.

17. Queen Noor, *Leap of Faith* (New York: Miramax Books, 2003).

18. Richard Fletcher, *The Cross and the Crescent: Christianity and Islam from Muhammad to the Reformation* (New York: Viking, 2004).

19. George W. Braswell, Jr., *What You Need to Know About Islam and Muslims* (Nashville, TN: Broadman & Holman, 2000).

20. George Grant, *The Blood of the Moon* (Nashville, TN: Nelson Books, 2001).

21. Josh McDowell and Don Douglas Stewart, *Handbook of Today's Religions* (Nashville, TN: Nelson Reference, 1992).

CHAPTER 6: EDUCATION
Recovering Our Lost Legacy

1. Horton Jennings, *Education and Wisdom* (New York: Tantamount Academic Press, 1977), 88.

2. Ibid., 89.

3. 1 Corinthians 8:1, KJV.

4. John Henry Newman, *The Idea of a University* (Chicago, IL: Loyola University, 1927), v.

5. Phoebe Courtney, *Target: America's Children* (Littleton, CO: Independent American, 1989), 14.

6. Francis DelVoe, *Education in Crisis* (Denver, CO: Littlefield, 1990), 200.

7. Ibid.

8. Ibid.

9. Ibid.

10. Ibid.; William Bennett, *The De-Valuing of America* (New York: Summit, 1992), 42; Thomas Sowell, *Inside American Education: The Decline the Deception, the Dogmas* (New York: Free Press, 1993).

11. Sowell, *Inside American Education.*

12. Bennett, *The De-Valuing of America,* 42–44.

13. Ibid.

14. Ibid.

15. Ibid.

16. Ibid.

17. Ibid.

18. Ibid.

19. *Education Reporter*, November 1993.

20. Ibid.

21. *Forbes*, June 7, 1993.

22. Dan Alexander, *Who's Running Our Schools? The Case Against the NEA Teacher Union* (Washington, DC: Save Our Schools, 1988), 7.

23. Ibid., 6.

24. Ibid.

25. Ibid.

26. Courtney, *Target: America's Children*, 15.

27. Ibid.

28. Ibid., 16.

29. *The Tennessean*, November 18, 1993.

30. Ibid.

31. Charles Spurgeon, *John Plowman's Talks* (London: Baptist Union Press, 1977), 79.

32. George Grant, "Dumb Certainties—National Education Association," *The Family Under Siege*, Liahona Learning Center, http://www.liahona-homeschooling.com/articles/dumbcertainties.html.

33. Ibid.

34. Clyde Hansen, *Poetry and Education*, (London: Underhills, 1996), ix.

35. Proverbs 1:2–7.

36. *Forbes*, June 7, 1993.

37. Ibid.

38. Alexander, *Who's Running Our Schools?*, 89.

39. *Forbes*, June 7, 1993.

40. Ibid.

41. *Tennessee Education Review*, July 1993.

42. Ibid.

43. Ibid.

44. Ibid.

45. Courtney, *Target: America's Children*, 51.

46. *Tennessee Education Review,* July 1993.

47. Ibid.

48. Ibid.

49. Ibid.

50. Ibid.

51. Samuel Blumenfeld, *NEA: Trojan Horse in American Education* (Boise, ID: Paradigm, 1984), x.

52. Os Guinness, *The Journey* (Colorado Springs, CO: NavPress, 2001), 45.

53. Lionel Ceveada, *Spanish Literature of the Sixteenth Century* (New York: Longmans Press, 1967), 248.

54. John 8:32.

55. This booklet is published by Focus on the Family and is available at http://www.family.org/resources/itempg.cfm?itemid=1399&refcd=CE0 4XSIRC&tvar=n.

56. Samuel Blumenfeld, *NEA: Trojan Horse in American Education* (Houston, TX: Paradigm Company, 1984).

CHAPTER 7: LIFE
Inalienable Rights, Irreplaceable People

1. Thomas Paine, *Common Sense and Other Essays* (New York: Signet Classics, 1977), 19.

2. George Grant, ed., *The Pocket Patriot* (Nashville, TN: Cumberland House, 2000), 41.

3. Ibid., 41–43.

4. Harold K. Lane, *Liberty! Cry Liberty!* (Boston: Lamb & Lamb Tractarian Society, 1939), 31.

5. Abraham Lincoln, *Speeches, Letters, and Papers: 1860–1864* (Washington, DC: Capitol Library, 1951), 341–342.

6. John W. Whitehead, *The Separation Illusion* (Milford, MI: Mott Media, 1977), 21.

7. Mike Huckabee, *Kids Who Kill* (Nashville, TN: Broadman and Holman, 1998), 51.

8. Lt. Col. Dave Grossman, *On Killing: The Psychological Cost of Learning to Kill in War and Society* (Boston, MA: Little Brown and Co., 1995), 3.

9. Ibid., xxix.

10. Ibid.

11. Ibid., 27.

12. Robert Bork, *Slouching Toward Gomorrah* (New York: ReganBooks, 1996), 182.

13. Ibid.

14. Ibid., 185.

15. Ibid.

16. George Grant, *Grand Illusions: The Legacy of Planned Parenthood* (Nashville, TN: Cumberland House, 2000), 24–25.

17. Ibid., 21.

18. Madeline Gray, *Margaret Sanger: A Biography* (New York: Marek, 1979), 326.

19. PPFA, "Annual Report," 21.

20. Grant, *Grand Illusions*, 25.

21. Planned Parenthood Federation of America, "2001 Service Report," 20.

22. Grant, *Grand Illusions*, 25.

23. Ibid.

24. *Austin American-Statesman*, November 22, 1993.

25. Life Decisions International Caleb Report, October 1993.

26. *Wall Street Journal*, July 19, 1993.

27. *New York Times*, June 19, 1993.

28. Planned Parenthood Federation of America, "A Risky Business: Reproductive Health Care in Litigation," 1988.

29. *New York Times*, June 19, 1993.

30. Scott Somerville, ed., *The Link Between Abortion and Breast Cancer* (Purcellville, VA: AIM, 1993).

31. Grant, *Grand Illusions*, iv.

32. Planned Parenthood Federation of America, "1981 Annual Report," 16.

33. Grant, *Grand Illusions*, 89.

34. Louis Harris, *American Teens Speak* (New York: Planned Parenthood Federation of America, 1986), 6.

35. Ibid., 7.

36. *Family Planning Perspectives*, July/August 1986.

37. Roberta Weiner, ed., *Teen Pregnancy: Impact on the Schools* (Alexandria, VA: Capitol Publications, 1987, 1994, 2000), 17.

38. Ibid.

39. Ibid.

40. Harris, *American Teens Speak*, 7.

41. John Ensor, *Answering the Call: Saving Innocent Lives, One Woman at a Time* (Colorado Springs, CO: Focus on the Family, 2003).

42. Figures are based on cumulative statistics provided by the U.S. Centers for Disease Control, *National Vital Statistics Report*, vol. 47, no. 29.

43. Alan Keyes, *Our Character, Our Future* (Grand Rapids, MI: Zondervan, 1996), 6.

44. Bruce Cook, *Parents, Teens and Sex: The Big Talk Book* (Atlanta, GA: Choosing the Best Publishing, 2003).

45. John Ensor, *Answering the Call* (Colorado Springs, CO: Focus on the Family, 2003).

46. Randy Alcorn, *Prolife Answers to Prochoice Arguments* (Sisters, OR: Multnomah, 2000).

47. George Grant, *Grand Illusions: The Legacy of Planned Parenthood* (Nashville, TN: Cumberland House Publishing, 2000).

48. George Grant, *The Micah Mandate* (Chicago: Moody Press, 1995).

CHAPTER 8: MEDIA
The Enemy in Our Midst

1. W. B. Yeats, "Meditations in Time of Civil War."

2. Bork, *Slouching Toward Gomorrah*, 179.

3. Press release, "Miller Delivers Floor Speech on 'Deficit of Decency' in America," February 12, 2004, http://miller.senate.gov/press/2004/02-12 -04decency.html.

4. Ibid.

5. Family Safe Media, Pornography Statistics 2003, www .familysafemedia.com/pornography_statistics.html.

6. Ibid.

7. Quoted in Huckabee, *Kids Who Kill*, 78.

8. *Media Analysis,* April 2003.

9. Ibid.

10. Ibid.

11. Ibid.

12. Neil Postman, *Amusing Ourselves to Death* (New York: Penguin, 1985), 155–156.

13. Ibid., vii–viii.

14. Ibid.

15. David Chagall, *Surviving the Media Jungle* (Nashville, TN: Broadman and Holman, 1996), 75.

16. William Bennett, *Index of Leading Cultural Indicators* (New York: Simon and Schuster, 1994), 103.

17. Ibid.

18. Ibid.

19. Ibid.

20. *Media Analysis*, May 1997.

21. Bennett, *Index of Leading Cultural Indicators*, 104.

22. Chagall, *Surviving the Media Jungle*, 89.

23. *Media Analysis*, May 1997.

24. Bennett, *Index of Leading Cultural Indicators*, 105.

25. Ibid.

26. Ibid., 106.

27. Chagall, *Surviving the Media Jungle*, 141.

28. *Media Analysis*, May 1997.

29. Ibid.

30. Bennett, *Index of Leading Cultural Indicators*, 110.

31. Ibid., 145.

32. Ibid., 142.

33. Ibid., 143.

34. Ibid.

35. Ibid.

36. Ibid.

37. Ibid.

38. Ibid.

39. Ibid.

40. Ibid., 144.

41. Ibid.

42. Ibid.

43. Ibid.

44. Ibid.

45. Ibid.

46. *Media Analysis*, May 1997.

47. Huckabee, *Kids Who Kill*, 80.

48. Bork, *Slouching Toward Gomorrah*, 124.

49. Bennett, *Index of Leading Cultural Indicators*, 112.

50. Ibid.

51. Ibid., 113–114.

52. Abraham Kuyper, *Observations* (London: English Standard, 1912), 119.

53. John Buchan, *Sundry Occasions* (Toronto: Collins, 1940), 201.

54. Adeline Lang, *The Loss of Civility* (New York: Walter Frasier, 1995), 34.

55. Ibid.

56. Ibid.

57. Christine Ammer, *The American Heritage Dictionary of Idioms* (Boston: Houghton Mifflin Co., 1997), as quoted in Dictionary.com, s.v. "fifth column," http://dictionary.reference.com/search?q=fifth+column.

58. Eudora Welty, *The Writing Life* (Oxford: The Center for Southern Culture, 1999), 2.

59. Daniel Boorstin, *The Image: A Guide to Pseudo-Events in America* (Vintage; September 1, 1992).

60. Michael Medved, *Hollywood vs. America* (San Francisco, CA: Harpercollins, 1992).

EPILOGUE:
Not Just a Dream, but a Vision

1. T. E. Lawrence, *Seven Pillars of Wisdom* (N.p.: Amereon Limited, 1935).

2. This quote appears in a number of wordings in various sources. Niemoeller spoke many times and at various places in his postwar travels, and he often concluded his speaking engagements in the United States with these words. Because of this, the wording may have changed slightly in his various speeches.

3. Jewish Virtual Library, s.v. "Martin Niemoeller (1892–1984)," http://www.jewishvirtuallibrary.org/jsource/biography/niemoeller.html.